LOVE, MARRIAGE, AND FAMILY

Learning from the Early Christians

ERKKI KOSKENNIEMI

CONCORDIA PUBLISHING HOUSE · SAINT LOUIS

PRAISE FOR *LOVE, MARRIAGE, AND FAMILY*

It is tempting to think that our present struggles on the subjects of sexuality, marriage, children, divorce, and other such related issues are charting new territory for Christians in society. Erkki Koskenniemi provides us with substantial evidence that the early church, following their Jewish heritage, confronted similar challenges. What they confronted and how they dealt with it, as spelled out in this book, provide much needed help as we stand, and live, in the confession of God's Word.

—**DAVID SHADDAY**,
PASTOR, ST. PAUL'S LUTHERAN CHURCH,
INDIANAPOLIS, INDIANA; AUTHOR OF
RECLAIMING THE HEART OF MARRIAGE

Published by Concordia Publishing House
3558 S. Jefferson Ave., St. Louis, MO 63118-3968
1-800-325-3040 • cph.org

Manufactured in the United States of America

---

1 2 3 4 5 6 7 8 9 10 34 33 32 31 30 29 28 27 26 25

CONTENTS

Foreword

Like most pastors, I have always found conversations with couples preparing for marriage to be difficult as well as joyous. More often than not, I have had to ask whether they are already living together and engaging in sexual relations without God's blessing. The goal is not to shame or condemn them but to seek the best possible foundation for their marriage. And that sometimes involves repentance, forgiveness, and the commitment to a fresh start. The next nervous conversation is usually about the marriage ceremony itself—a struggle to keep it focused on Christ and worshipful in character without importing shallow secular music or the latest Hollywood fads. And then, of course, there is the inevitable discomfort over the traditional wedding vows, whether the bride will be willing to say "obey."

These premarital discussions involve a clash of cultures, but not in the way many couples perceive it. Is the church simply clinging to old-fashioned notions of marriage, women, and sexuality? The truth is rather the opposite. As this deceptively simple book details the ways in which love, marriage, and family operated in the ancient Greco-Roman world, it quickly becomes apparent that the world around us is, in many ways, more "traditional" than the Christian Church. As Christian influence on Western culture wanes, our culture is not so much pursuing a sexual revolution as it is simply returning to the ways of the ancient world.

Thus the reader should not be surprised to find in the following pages that the beliefs and practices of people in the ancient world are strikingly modern, including the widespread use of contraception, abortion, and exposure of infants so that men could engage in sexual exploits without taking responsibility for their actions; cultural expectation that boys should become sexually active as soon as they were physically capable but not commit to marriage until many years later; sex as entertainment; children as a burden; and the cultural normalization of homosexual activity, exploitation of young boys and vulnerable women, frivolous divorce, and multiple remarriages.

Erkki Koskenniemi, a sparkling classicist and philologist who is also widely known in Finland for teaching the faith to generations of young Lutherans in confirmation camp, is eminently qualified to be our guide to this ancient world. He is one of the few people I know whose name appears in the footnotes of the standard Greek lexicon of the New Testament (Bauer, Danker, Amdt, Gingrich, editors)—together with the name of his more famous father, Heikki. His doctoral dissertation on Apollonius of Tyana debunked the mighty Rudolf Bultmann by exposing the mythological character of his own scholarship. (That's an inside joke for New Testament specialists, by the way.)

Dr. Koskenniemi shows us that the clash of cultures was never simply between old-fashioned notions and progressive ideologies but has always been between God's Word and the way of the sinful world. He unpacks the teachings of the Old Testament, which gave God's people a holy and righteous way to live, love, marry, and bear children. And he demonstrates how the apostolic writers of the New Testament strengthened Christian people to live out their holy lives in the midst of a rebellious culture. By the strength of God's Word, we can do the same today.

In my premarital instruction, I have always tried to confront and deconstruct the false and dangerous notions of our contemporary culture by walking through the three great texts in our marriage rite: God's institution of marriage at the creation of Adam and Eve in Genesis 1–2, our Lord's reaffirmation of the goodness of marriage in Matthew 19, and Paul's Christological exposition of marriage in Ephesians 5. While these texts and the Christian way of life they describe can bestow the blessing of a healthy, long-lived marriage in accord with God's will, Ephesians 5 crowns this Christian catechesis with a great Gospel blessing. For Paul teaches us that a great mystery is hidden in this seemingly mundane institution: "I am saying that it refers to Christ and the church" (v. 32). Yes, it's about the Gospel! The ordered relationship of man and wife certainly isn't about power and self-gratification, nor even just about domestic harmony and mutual care. Rather, there is an opportunity in a Christian marriage for a husband to proclaim Christ to his bride through his self-sacrificial love, as "Christ is the head of the church, His body, and is Himself its Savior" (v. 23). And a wife can grow in faith and model it to her husband as she willingly subordinates herself to him "as the church submits to Christ" (v. 24).

This is the glory of marriage when illuminated by the light of God's Word. This is what the Christian Church can offer to men and women seeking to deepen and bless their union and the children God may give them. It has always been a countercultural message because it comes from God's wisdom, not man's. I hope and pray that this little book will guide the church in exploring this sacred mystery and strengthen her confession before a world that needs God's blessing as much as ever.

THOMAS M. WINGER,
PRESIDENT, CONCORDIA LUTHERAN THEOLOGICAL SEMINARY,
ST. CATHARINES, ONTARIO, CANADA

PREFACE

As a pastor and Bible teacher for decades, my favorite part of my work has been working with young Christians. Over the years, they have faced many challenges growing up in the modern Western world. Many of them have gotten married and raised children. I have enjoyed knowing their families and sharing their journey. When I see the mess in which especially younger people must live in our world, my heart praises God, who still guides us with His Word in this world.

Before studying theology, I spent years studying Greek and Latin texts. As a biblical scholar, I often return to these works. I learned to love tragedians like Sophocles and Euripides, poets like Virgil and Horace, and many other writers. While I admired their insight into the human mind and their strong morals, I did not agree with all of their views. Greek and Roman morals often clashed with Jewish and Christian ethics regarding sex, family, and marriage.

Today I encounter people who hold stunningly similar ideas in a post-Christian world. The views of reasoning Gentiles on subjects like abortion, premarital sexual activity, homosexuality, marriage, affairs, and divorce were not all that different from the views of today's reasoning Westerners. My favorite poets weren't hopelessly evil, nor are the people I encounter today; they, like the ancients, simply lack biblical guidance, and that makes them think and do what society commonly considers reasonable. You may wonder what ancient Greece and Rome can teach us about the world we live in. In the Old and New Testaments, we meet God's people, who struggled to follow God's standard despite the world's ungodly standards. Today

I also meet Christians who, though decreasing in number, still strive to follow biblical standards.

This book explores traditional family morals among Greeks and Romans. It also shows how Jews and, subsequently, early Christians lived as minorities. We have much to learn by studying the world in which they lived. It is time to study our roots, present our treasures, and call everyone to hear the loving voice of the Creator. He once gave, and still gives, forgiveness and a home for people who had earlier lived a completely different life. This is a book about our loving God, who has given us love, marriage, and family—the best gifts we can have in this world—and who also tells us how to use those gifts.

At the time I was finalizing this book, I celebrated the forty-fifth anniversary of my marriage with Marja. God has given us five sons, lovely daughters-in-law, and—at this point—twelve lively grandchildren. After these decades, I indeed recognize that this is the best that sinful people like us can have in this world. I thankfully dedicate this book to Marja, knowing that nothing is better than to love and be loved until death separates us and makes us wait for the voice of our merciful God, who will reunite us with all the saints in His glory.

INTRODUCTION

Our first Christian sisters and brothers lived as a minority in the cities and among the people of the Roman Empire. In many ways, the lives they lived are of interest to contemporary Christians. What kind of difficulties, for instance, did a young Christian mother in Corinth face when explaining her family choices to her neighbors? What were the differences a Christian pupil at school had to repeatedly explain to his friends, who still did not quite understand him? What was life like for a Christian slave girl, a stranger in her own city? Observing religious feasts in Gentile temples was an essential part of social life, a kind of national pastime, and whoever refused to join the crowd was easily suspected, if not hated. However, for Christians, participation was at odds with their faith. But perhaps the single biggest difference between Christians and their neighbors was sexual morality. It was also a very important factor in drawing theological lines that continue to shape our thinking. This booklet illuminates early Christian sexual morality in its historical context and asks what we can learn from the choices of early Christians.

So, what was the sexual morality of Gentile Corinth? How similar was it to the practice of the rest of the Greek and Roman world? We have some of those answers, but not all of them. The period we know as classical antiquity lasted more than a thousand years. Not surprisingly, ethics, morals, and practices varied over that time, and there was no common ancient sexual morality. Furthermore, the Mediterranean world was a sea of different people, and we know next to nothing about many of them, and even less about their sexual morality.

GREEK AND ROMAN SOURCES

Even when we have good sources, it is unclear what sweeping generalizations we can make. There are numerous texts, for example, from the golden age of Athens, the dialogues of Plato, the tragedies of Euripides, and numerous speeches at courts that richly describe life in the city. All of these texts, however, tend to express the views more of the wealthy elite, poets and philosophers, and less those of ordinary people. And less than two hundred kilometers away in Sparta, people led completely different lives.

Luckily, there are other kinds of sources. The Greeks living in Egypt left behind papyri that allow us glimpses of ordinary life back then. Promissory notes, petitions directed to officials, marriage contracts, and other documents were preserved to us only by chance, and many of them tell us about the lives of ordinary people.

Roman and Latin texts draw a different picture. Many literary texts have been preserved, but we also receive some help from papyri, though little. In addition, as in the Greek-speaking areas, there are thousands of inscriptions or texts carved in stones. Although these are of limited assistance—you may ask how little of our lives will be written in stone—they provide important pieces of the puzzle. There is also graffiti, for example in Pompeii, that we may compare to scribbles and ugly drawings in public bathrooms today.

So Athens, Egypt, Corinth, and Rome tell one set of stories. But who can say anything about the world Paul and Barnabas encountered when they arrived among the Lycaonians, whose language was as unknown to them as to modern scholars? There were numerous people whose language and culture are almost completely unknown to us. Generalization would thus be dangerous.

Jewish Sources

But the first Christians were not the first to stand out from their Gentile neighbors in their manner of life. Jews had lived in Palestine for centuries, but millions of them also lived in Diaspora in various parts of the Mediterranean. Their families, communities, and synagogues made up a distinct way of life. The rich world of early Judaism helps us understand what it meant to live as a minority. This Jewish tradition shaped Christian thinking as well.

Judaism in Jesus' time was by no means a monolithic religion, as we can already see in the differences between the Pharisees and Sadducees in the Gospels. We do not know exactly what the Sadducees, Pharisees, and scribes taught. The large collections of Mishna and Tosefta,[1] as well as other rabbinic sources, include traditions that were added much later, and these traditions originate from a variety of sources, time periods, and cultural environments. Moreover, early Jewish texts, written in both Semitic languages, like the so-called Old Testament Apocrypha and the Scrolls from Qumran, and in Greek, like the works by Philo and Josephus, show that early Judaism had room for a plethora of opinions. Recent scholars even claim that Jews lived like the people around them. It would indeed be naïve to claim that every Jew followed the standards of Jewish teachers. Nevertheless, the scarce sources we have tell us that religious teachers tried to teach a special manner of life. The role of the synagogue as the place where ethics were taught should never be overlooked.

Alexandria, which was one of the most important cities in the world and a famous cultural center, had a strong Jewish

1 The Mishna is an early collection of Jewish teachings, redacted at the end of the second Christian century. The Tosefta is a corpus of supplementary materials to the Mishna, redacted between AD 200 and 400.

minority, a number of whom went to the best schools in the city. Usually, many people were allowed to live in a city, but only a tiny minority could become citizens. These people were trained in a gymnasium, which was not merely a school, but rather a military service sorting the future citizens. The life of a Jew in an Alexandrian gymnasium differed from the life of a farmer in a small Palestinian village or a merchant in Philippi, where the few Jews living in the town did not even have a synagogue. Some Jews probably fully adopted the Gentile manner of life, some rejected it, and some adopted parts of it—as people always do. It seems, however, that in general, Jews in the Mediterranean world followed their Jewish way and tried to teach it to their offspring. It is difficult and often impossible to say how much ordinary Jews listened to their teachers. Notwithstanding, it is important to trace the sexual morality these teachers tried to teach to the people who cared to listen.

Early Christian Sources

Jewish heritage greatly influenced the early church, but the sources are very limited when it comes to understanding the lives of the first Christians. Outside of the Bible, there is very little material from the end of the first and the beginning of the second century AD. There are more sources from the second half of the second century, but it does not take very long to read every Christian text written before AD 200. After this time, the number goes up, and it would take a lifetime to read them all. Unfortunately, there are fewer documents shedding light on the lives of ordinary Christian people. For example, only Paul's letters testify of early Christian life in Corinth. Based on them, sparks were flying in the Christian community, which was clearly struggling with the sexual morality of Corinth. Understanding conventional Greek and Jewish ways of life helps us understand these struggles and the solutions Paul offers. That alone is enough to make our journey worthwhile as Christians struggle with the sexual morality of our own culture.

Many scholars claim that Christianity brought little or nothing new to Mediterranean ethics. This might be true, but it only concerns the wider range of ethics, not the narrow range of sexual morals. Most moral teachers tell you to do good deeds and avoid bad ones, and this was certainly common to both Christian and Gentile teachers. A closer look, of course, reveals the differences. Hardly anywhere did the Jewish and Christian morals differ as much from conventional Greek and Roman thought than in the field of family and sexual morals.

Exploring the New Testament gives new perspectives to all Christians who are seeking God's will in their own life. It might be an exaggeration to say there is nothing new under the sun, but for the most part, our difficulties are not unique to our time. The world was not an easy place for the first Christians to live. What can we learn from the challenges they faced?

Reflection Questions

- What expectations do you have for your study group or self-study?

- How well do you think you know the family ethics within early Christian families?

- How well do you know the world of the Old Testament, early Judaism, and the Greek and Roman worlds?

1

A Child Is Born. What Next?

A typical family in ancient Rome was strikingly similar to a typical family in our time. Families often didn't have more than three children. A whole family would have fit nicely in a modern car. In this chapter, we will take a look at how family planning was done in ancient times. Contraception will be addressed in chapter 7.

In ancient Greece and Rome, family planning was simple. An unwelcomed child was either killed or exposed. This was apparently a well-known practice for everyone in ancient days, and it appears in mythology (Oedipus, Romulus and Remus) and historical sources.

In general, the life of a person living in the ancient world was divided into two areas. Some things were ruled by the government, and some things were ruled by the individual. The birth of children and the size of the family belonged to the area ruled by the individual. The laws rarely, if ever, limited the exposure of children. Governments often hoped for bigger families, but it was the challenges of everyday life that led people to make their own family decisions. The typical family was quite small because few parents made room for more than two sons and one daughter. Other children born to them outside of marriage were not allowed to join the family. Since child mortality was very high (perhaps about 30 percent or more), we do not know how many children were exposed. Some abandoned children survived, but regrettably, there aren't any statistics on their number.

Child Exposure

The reasons children were exposed were pretty similar in Greece and Rome. If a child was born under bad omens, from the wrong father, was of the wrong sex, or suffered a disability, he or she was often abandoned. Poor people did not have enough money to feed all of their babies, and wealthy families did not want to divide their property between too many children. When a child was born after the planned number of babies had been born, or when a child was simply not needed, that baby was not welcome, and it was either killed or exposed. The fate of exposed children varied from sunlight to dark shadows: Often, cold, hunger, or beasts ended the tender life during the child's first days. If the mother knew of a wealthy, childless couple who desperately needed a family member, she might leave her newborn by their door so that they would raise the child as their own. Some exposed babies were brought to brothels to be raised as sex slaves. But most of the children who survived being exposed were probably raised to serve as slaves in neighboring villages.

Exposing children sounds really cruel. But it should be noted that parents didn't rejoice in exposing or killing their children. It was considered a sad necessity. Greeks and Romans whispered about distant people who never abandoned their children. They greatly honored those people. Some of those people were far enough away to serve as moral examples, and good storytellers added impressive tales about their manners.

Jewish Views on Infanticide

But Greeks and Romans also knew of a group of people living in their midst who did not abandon their children. For Jews, abandoning children was strictly forbidden. They viewed it as one of the sins they were never allowed to commit. Exposing babies is not explicitly addressed or unequivocally banned in the Mosaic Law, but early Jewish teachers clearly forbade it. The ban was included in several summaries of the Mosaic Law in the first century AD, especially by Philo, Josephus, and Pseudo-Phocylides.

Of course, banning something doesn't always prevent people from doing it. Sometimes, a newborn child was found abandoned in a Jewish town. That always raised the question, Is this child a Jew or not? Teachers might say that she or he was, provided that the majority of inhabitants in that town were Jews. However, Rabbi Judah, an influential teacher from the second century AD, said that the child belonged to the majority of those who abandoned babies. In other words, the child was a Gentile because Jewish parents did not abandon their children (Mishna, *Makhshirin* 2:7).

Early Christian Views on Infanticide

Even though a clear ban on exposure is not included in either the Old or New Testament, the early church adopted Jewish customs very quickly. Soon after the New Testament was written, the first Christian works followed, word for word, part of a Jewish moral summary now lost. The *Epistle of Barnabas*, written soon after AD 100, and the *Didache*, written only some decades later, use identical words:

> You shall not abort a child nor, again, commit infanticide. (*Epistle of Barnabas* 19:5)[2]

> You shall not abort a child or commit infanticide. (*Didache* 2:2)

The earliest Christian writings make it clear that the Jews had gotten this one right. The first Christians followed the Jewish teachings for centuries, both in the East and in the West. Two of the most influential teachers, Basil the Great in the East (AD 330–379) and Augustine of Hippo in the West (AD 354–430), finally also made it part of Christian doctrine almost unanimously honored to our day. Basil, who defended weak and poor people, was adamant and ruled that parents who had exposed their child had to repent for no less than twenty years before they could be admitted to Holy Communion. Only extreme poverty shifted the guilt to wealthy people. After all, if poor people had to expose their children because they could not feed them, their rich neighbors should have had compassion and helped them (*Epistle of Basil the Great,* 217:56). In the fourth century, Christians were known for saving and raising exposed children.

The first Christians adopted almost all of the arguments from their Jewish predecessors. It was easy to describe the terrible fate of abandoned babies: Hunger and cold killed many, and some were eaten by wild animals who regularly visited the dung heaps where the babies were left. Christian writers helped the parents picture how their abandoned offspring became slaves or were mutilated by their masters so they would get more money when begging on the streets.

2 Michael W. Holmes, ed. and trans., *The Apostolic Fathers: Greek Texts and English Translations*, 3rd ed. (Baker Academic, 2007).

The worst part of their terrible vision included the thought of a father visiting brothels and unknowingly going into his own daughter or son whom he had abandoned as a child. But the most important argument was the Fifth Commandment, "You shall not murder," which prevented killing newborns. This teaching was conventional among Jews in Jesus' time. We may call it "a tradition of the elders." Christians immediately learned to equate exposure of infants with killing. Almighty God has created every human being, and that means that every child has the right to live.

ANCIENT VIEWS ON ABORTION

Ancient sources speak about abortion, but they don't explain much about how it was performed. It was easiest to do it early and with drugs—if they worked. For a long time, scholars used to laugh at the ancients who thought these drugs could be effective, but not anymore. Modern tests with animals have shown that ancient medicaments very effectively caused abortions, and although they have not been tested on humans, their effect is indisputable (see ch. 7). The famous Hippocratic oath is very critical of abortion, but we aren't aware of any actual ancient laws that banned it. Since exposure was fully legal, it certainly limited the number of embryotomies (surgical removal of the embryo), which were always dangerous. Nonetheless, both drugs and embryotomy were legal for Greeks and Romans. Sources do not allow us to distinguish abortion by drugs from contraception among Jews and Christians, but embryotomy is sometimes mentioned.

Jewish teachers strictly banned abortion, and this ban was a common part of Jewish ethical handbooks (e.g., Philo, *On the Special Laws*, 3:117–19; Pseudo-Phocylides, 184–85; Josephus, *Apion*, 2.199–203). On ethical handbooks, see chapter 3. However, if abortion was needed to save the life of the mother, it was allowed.

> The woman who is in hard labor—they chop up the child in her womb and they remove it limb by limb, because her life takes precedence over his life. (Mishna, *Ohalot* 7:6)

The Tosefta, collected clearly after the Mishna, repeats the rule and adds that the operation had to be performed even if it was a Sabbath day (Tosefta, *Yebamot* 9:5). That it required the decision of a court shows how seriously the case was taken. Moreover, the right to this emergency abortion ended at a certain moment:

> If its greater part has gone forth, they do not touch him, for they do not set aside one life on account of another life. (Mishna, *Ohalot* 7:6)[3]

Jewish teachers thus allowed abortion to save the life of the mother, but they set clear limits. The life of the child was to be saved, if possible. Man is not free to do with the child whatever he wants, but he is bound by the Law of God.

Early Christian Views on Abortion

The early church closely followed its Jewish heritage. The *Epistle of Barnabas* and the *Didache* agree word for word, also here following the lost Jewish ethical handbooks:

3 Jacob Neusner, *The Mishnah: A New Translation* (Yale University Press, 1991).

> You shall not abort a child or commit infanticide. (*Didache* 2:2)
>
> You shall not abort a child nor, again, commit infanticide. (*Epistle of Barnabas* 19:5)[4]

The *Apocalypse of Peter*, written between AD 100 and 180, harshly describes the posthumous punishment awaiting parents who had aborted their children (8:1–10), and Clement of Alexandria joins this tradition (*Eclogae*, 41; *GCS*, 17:149). It is often difficult to determine whether writers speak of contraception or abortion or both, because the same drugs were used for both purposes. Nonetheless, abortion, exposure, and the killing of newborn children were strictly banned by Christians, according to early Christian writings. Although abortion was generally banned, Christians also allowed that it was permitted to save the life of the mother. It was, in the words of Tertullian (AD 160–220), "a sad necessity" (*De anima*, 25:4), and Augustine accepted it too (*Enchiridion*, 86).

The Right to Choose

First Jews, and then Christians following them, took their own way based on God's Word and banned abortion and the exposure of infants. The heated modern debate about abortion especially focuses on one question: Does the individual (the mother) or the government have the right to decide the fate of a fetus? In Greek and Roman societies, there was no doubt about the answer: It was the individual's (the father's) decision, and the government had nothing to say if the family decided to expose its newborn child. Statesmen could be worried about the small number of children and indeed tried

4 Holmes, *The Apostolic Fathers.*

to support families with different programs, as Augustus did. However, the family always made the decision. Jews and Christians thought differently. In their opinion, neither the individual, as in the Greek and Roman environment, nor the government, as in traditional Christian countries, had the right to decide on the life and death of the fetus or the newborn child. This right belonged to God, and every human being had to follow His will.

This case calls us to look at the past, but it also calls us to look at the modern world and the countries in the world that have no Christian traditions. For more than a thousand years, the Western world followed this Christian tradition and banned abortion and the exposure of infants. Today, Western culture has widely accepted abortion, but most of us are still unaware of what selective abortions and killing newborns mean in Asia, where people strongly prefer sons to daughters. Scholars have created a term, *gendercide*, derived from *gender* and *genocide*. At worst, it means that due to selective abortions and exposures, only 100 girls are born in a region, compared to 136 boys. This has caused young men to strongly outnumber young women, and it is hard to even understand the consequences. About one hundred million women have been aborted or exposed as infants in the area from Armenia to China. It would be easy to point to the Chinese government and its one-child policy, but this is only a part of the truth. While the government has abandoned this policy, people in China, as well as in many other Asian countries, still prefer sons to daughters. The daughter married to a new family is expected to take care of her parents-in-law. An Indian proverb states that whoever raises a girl waters an alien garden. This raises moral questions, as well as questions about the future of that society. The next decades will show what happens in a society where millions of young men seek wives in vain. Apparently, governments will try to turn the terrible trend around. Unfortunately, the past teaches the lesson that laws and programs can hardly beat common values.

Both the Jews and subsequently the Christians considered the birth of a child a result of God's creation, as formulated, for example, in Psalm 139:13–15:

> For You formed my inward parts;
> You knitted me together in my mother's womb.
> I praise You, for I am fearfully and wonderfully made
> Wonderful are Your works;
> my soul knows it very well.
> My frame was not hidden from You,
> when I was being made in secret,
> intricately woven in the depths of the earth.

Similar words in the Psalms are most intimately connected with the actual life of the psalmist. A person in fear and danger is turning to his Creator and humbly praying for help from the One who has given him life (e.g., Psalm 22:10; Job 10:11). Every human being has been created by God, which is why she or he is unique. Everyone, including a small child before her or his birth, has a mighty defender. This belief essentially differed from common values in the Greek and Roman world, where the fate of a child was decided by the family, or, to be exact, by the father. In later Christian societies, this role was taken by the government and its laws. The trend during the last decades has been to give the right of the decision to the individual everywhere. The mission of the church is to proclaim that almighty God alone has the authority to decide on the life and death of human beings.

Reflection Questions

- What similarities are you finding between ancient and modern societies?

- Many cultures have permitted and still permit parents to abort or abandon their children because of their gender. Do you think this will also become a common practice in Western societies? If so, how do you think parents will be able to choose the gender of their child?

- To what extent should Christians try to influence the laws of their countries? To what extent should they focus on taking care of their Christian communities?

2

FAMILY FEASTS AND SOCIAL LIFE

Western Christian churches have struggled to pass on the faith to the next generations. They may find help from the church's Jewish roots. Ancient Jews understood the importance of having a sense of community in difficult times.

A newborn baby usually makes a family happy. But, as we have seen above, this wasn't always the case in ancient Rome, and the baby was far from safe. Unlike Greeks and Romans, first Jews and, subsequently, Christians banned the practices of abandoning or killing children, even if the parents felt they were a burden or needless. Now it is time to ask what happened soon after the birth of a child whose parents planned to keep and raise their child. It is time to speak about family feasts and simultaneously about the sense of community and its role in Christian sexual morality.

GREEK FAMILY FEASTS

We don't know much about the first weeks of a baby's life in ancient times, which shows how little we know about the everyday lives of ancient people. They certainly celebrated the birth of the baby, but we only have glimpses of these feasts. What happened in classical Athens was probably the usual occurrence elsewhere too. The Athenian people used to have a family feast on the tenth day (or, as some sources say, on the fifth), called *decate* or *amphidromia*. The name *amphidromia*, from "running around," reflects the original function of the feast. The child was apparently put forward for show, and the relatives formed a big circle and walked around the baby, or the midwives carried the child around among the relatives. The child was formally inspected and so taken into the family. The inspection was, of course, a mere formality because the parents had already screened the baby before the feast. Nevertheless, the family feast meant that the child was accepted into the family and received his or her name in this feast, which drastically changed his or her role in the family and among his or her relatives.

Roman Family Feasts

The Roman parallel of the Greek feast was called *lustratio*, in which the baby received his or her name. The father formally accepted the child by taking him or her in his arms (*tollere*). Religion, or at least religious practices, were strongly present during the baby's first days. The word *lustratio* refers to "cleaning," apparently to expel evil spirits. Plautus the comedian (ca. 255–184 BC), possibly following a Greek original as he often did, tells that people made sacrifices to gods the fifth day after a son was born (*Trucul.*, 423). Tertullian says that a holy meal was offered to Juno (that is, Hera) every day before the feast (*De anima*, 39). When the child entered the family, he also entered a religious community, although the practices may have been only traditional and without any deeper spiritual reflection.

If a newborn wasn't abandoned or killed, she was thus taken into a Greek or Roman family. Classical scholars sometimes distinguished between biological and sociological birth. A child's biological birth, and still less her conception, did not guarantee any right to life in the Greek or Roman world. It was the sociological birth, manifested in the family feast, the acceptance of the extended family, that gave the baby her place in the family and in society. It was easier to abandon or kill a child before he or she was taken into the family. Such a distinction would, however, have been alien to Jews. To them, biological birth meant being born into the world created by God and protected by Him. They believed that men should not extinguish the light given by God.

Jewish Family Feasts

Like the Greeks and the Romans, Jewish people also had their family feast when a child (son) was born. Abraham was told by God that he and all the males in his family who were eight days old should be circumcised (Genesis 17:9–14), and this rule was unequivocally repeated in Leviticus 12:3. The Maccabean revolt (see below in this chapter) made it clear that mainstream Judaism considered circumcision a necessity. It was something strictly required, and it distinguished between *us* and *them*. That is why Paul proudly says that he was circumcised on the eighth day (Philippians 3:4–5). We can assume that the rite was followed by a family feast, in which the son was taken into the family and religious community, as described in Luke 1:57–66 at the circumcision of John the Baptist.

THE SOCIAL DIMENSION OF RELIGION

In the ancient world, the line between individual and social life was drawn differently than it is today. Greco-Roman religiosity offered many options one could freely take or leave, but even a single conversion to Judaism in a city could lead to pogroms, violent riots. The social dimension of religion was much stronger than we understand it in the modern Western world, where individual freedom is a basic fundamental value. But looking at the situation between minorities and majorities in foreign countries can help us understand how different the world was in ancient times. A religion is not simply articles that people consider true. It is the very core of national identity. A convert from a minority religion abandons not only his former opinions but also his family, nation, and culture. Religion has never been only a set of dogmatic articles people believe. Judaism in Jesus' time was a good example of this. Despite all its diversity, it had a very strong social and national dimension. The Jewish people, mostly living in the minority among various peoples, had a strong national identity, marked by the Mosaic Law and the circumcision of male children. Religion and morals were taught in the synagogue, which was the heart of the local community.

The children of Abraham lived in contact with other peoples in the centuries before and after Christ, and the wealthier Jews especially heard the call of Greek culture. Was it indeed necessary to follow all the Mosaic rules and especially to require the circumcision of every male child? Was not Greek wisdom at many points compatible with Jewish views? Some Jews had slowly assimilated with Greek culture, and the so-called Hellenistic reform, which had strong support among the Jewish oligarchy, made this common in Jerusalem early in the second century BC. The Mosaic Law was not observed in detail, and circumcision was abandoned (1 Maccabees 1:15). But a strong rural movement combining religious arguments with secular ones canceled the reform and began a decades-long fight with non-Jewish overlords until independence was finally reached. After those events, the Torah and circumcision unequivocally belonged to Jewish identity, although, as always, some individuals took their own paths.

Jews started to go out from Palestine very early, well before the fall(s) of Jerusalem. They lived as a minority among Mediterranean people. Even when Jews were permitted to return to Jerusalem, many chose to remain outside Palestine. These minorities could be very strong; there were hundreds of thousands of Jews in Egypt, and in Rome, there were probably fifty thousand or even more. They were separated from other people because the Mosaic Law regulated what and with whom they ate and whom they married. The heart of a local Jewish community was its synagogue. When there were too few Jews in a town to have a synagogue, Jews used to gather for prayer on a riverside on the Sabbath, and that was where Paul knew to seek his fellow Jews (Acts 16:13). Whether they were a smaller or larger group, the only way to avoid total assimilation was to come together.

Early Christian Baptism

Various modern denominations disagree on the question of baptizing infants. It might be needless to thoroughly address this question here. Modern people struggle to accept the idea that parents should decide the religion of their children. Clearly, the sense of community was a much stronger factor in classical antiquity than in our times, and this strongly adds to biblical arguments that children and infants were to be baptized. When the father of a family converted to Christianity, this also meant that his whole family converted, including his children and slaves (Acts 11:14; 16:15; 18:8). It is more than probable that the first Christians replaced the Greek, Roman, or Jewish initiation rite and family feast with Christian Baptism, especially because Colossians 2:11–12 compares Baptism to circumcision.

If an individual converted to Christ in the first century AD, the radical step often meant troubles within his or her community, as clearly seen, for example, in 1 Peter. It was not easy to exit from the religious and possibly also the national community, especially if you were a slave. The process grew easier when the new religion started to form its own communities within local churches; in other words, families and extended families.

Thoughts for Our Age of Individualism

Family feasts thus connected individuals to common families, to networks of relatives, and to peoples. The Western world now lives in an age of individualization, and a sense of community is fading. The roles of family, relatives, and even nationality have been greatly reduced during the last fifty years, and this also influences our faith. Christianity has grown more and more private—my own faith, and often also my very personal bundle of ideas. Global Christianity is, however, anything but an individual endeavor. In Europe, refugees have arrived from the Near East, and many of them have found Christ here. They have taught us a different manner of life. Religion does not only mean that you consider certain ideas true. It also means that you belong to a community and join it with your friends. "You are our family now," a newly baptized young man said when his conversion meant that he had to cut the ties with his Muslim family. These people have taught us to read the New Testament with new eyes. Symbolic speech in the New Testament reflects the communal sense of the first Christians. The church is God's people, God's family, and the Body of Christ intimately connecting its different members.

Lacking a sense of community has certainly reduced our ability to pass down biblical family morals to the next generations. Mothers and fathers have all too often been left alone to fight against the flow our youth and young adults meet in media, classes, and locker rooms. This flow is too strong for a young individual, if not for grown-ups as well. To fight it, we need a community. We meet problems everywhere when Christian children miss contact with other Christian families, and when Christian teens do not know other teens who read the Bible. Without their synagogues and relatively unified instruction on what was wrong and right, Mediterranean Jews would have assimilated with majorities and disappeared well before Jesus, and the same is true with early Christians and their house churches. Western Christianity will lose the little it has left of Christian ethics unless the churches again start to be places where pastors encounter their members and call them to join the common path.

Reflection Questions

- Religion played a crucial role in ancient societies. How does it unify families, relatives, and nations today?

- Do we differentiate between biological and social birth? How?

- How can we enhance the social life within our churches to strengthen Christian family and sexual morals?

- Could a newcomer say to the members of your church, "You are our family now"? If not, what can be done to change that?

3

When Children Grow Up

The Mediterranean classical world was a sea of many different people, and it included various ideals, which changed over the centuries. That world cannot be summarized in a few pages. Nevertheless, it is possible to describe what was typical for Greek or Roman youth before marriage. We will start this chapter with young, free citizens and end it with slaves.

Customs for Young Women

Surprisingly, the typical path for girls differed from the one usual for boys, only for the simple reason that girls can get pregnant but boys cannot. That explains why girls usually married early, at about age 15, and their parents kept a close eye on them before then. In classical Athens, girls and women were expected to stay at home, literally inside the walls of the house (Sparta was different). Plutarch claims that Athenian fathers were allowed to sell their daughters into slavery if they were caught having premarital sex (Plutarch, *Solon*, 23:2). Lysias (ca. 445–380 BC) even claims in a speech written to defend an Athenian man in court that girls in his house had never seen males, aside from their family members. The rhetor may have exaggerated, but a girl raised in a free family could hardly have had premarital sex before her wedding day. And Lysias hardly exaggerated much, because Cornelius Nepos, a Roman writer (ca. 100–24 BC), still wondered why Greeks excluded their women from dinners, while Roman housewives used to eat together with guests.

Customs for Young Men

Young men took a drastically different path. Sources show that they visited slave girls and prostitutes as soon as they were physically able to have sex. Men typically married much later than women, at about 30 (see below), and they were usually well experienced in both heterosexual and homosexual relations before their wedding (see below). Plato, in his famous *Symposium*, made Alcibiades come late and drunk to the dinner. He had a flute on his arms and, as the rest of the guests had done, delivered a speech on love. Alcibiades certainly knew what he was speaking about. The time for marriage and lawful children was after the busy time of youth.

Aristotle seemed to formulate the Athenian convention by saying that men should beget children at 30, and sex before that had "other goals" (*De re publica*, 7:16, 1335b). Attic New Comedy[5] with stereotypical roles especially described those "other goals," typically making a wealthy father, his rascal son, and a pretty girl confused together before the happy end typical of the genre. Philosophers certainly warned that pleasure should not rule over a wise man. It was not a virtue for anyone that he was ruled by dice, food, wine, or any strong

5 Attic New Comedy was a form of ancient Greek theater that originated in Athens in the Hellenistic period after the death of Alexander the Great.

emotions, including sexual pleasure. Nevertheless, fathers or teachers rarely, if ever, limited the premarital sex of young men.

Sex with a young, free girl was a crime (*stuprum*) in Rome, and it led to trouble with her relatives. However, the sources show that the life of a boy between puberty and marriage was similar to a boy's life in the Greek world. He was expected to have numerous partners—or rather, to be exact, sex objects. Nevertheless, he was told to leave married women alone. Marcus Porcius Cato (234–149 BC) was, if anyone, an icon of Roman virtues. He arrived at the Floralia feast only to walk out conspicuously at the well-known and eagerly expected moment when the prostitutes stripped themselves and threw their clothes away (Martialis, 1. *Proemium*). Nevertheless, he approvingly greeted a young man coming from a brothel, saying that it was a much better choice than the bed of a married woman, when a man covets a woman (Horace, *Epistles*, 1.2:31–35).

Male Sexuality

Married men did not have to resort to pursuing married women. They owned their slave girls and were free to use them. If banquets or baths did not offer enough options, brothels were ready to serve customers. The famous building dug out of volcanic ash in Pompeii with menus and prices witnesses the market available for anyone. The quickest and cheapest option was to go to homeless people and take a woman in a *fornix*, "vault," which is recalled by the term *fornication*.

So, the market indeed served young men as well as older men. Marcus Tullius Cicero, the famous advocate and statesman (106–43 BC), defended a young man by referring to the *ludus* period (a time for casual, noncommittal sexual experience) and the numerous partners belonging to it (*Cael.*, 28).

Marcus Varro (116–27 BC) encouraged young men to fully enjoy *ludus*, which allowed them so much enjoyment (*Men.*, 87). Late antiquity tended to appreciate ascetic ideals here as in other areas more than the earlier period. Nevertheless, I do not know of any teacher saying that a Roman man should be a virgin until marriage. As said, people in late antiquity generally emphasized a disciplined manner of life more than in earlier times, and it also influenced sexual morals. But premarital sex and numerous partners were not shameful and especially not considered a sin as long as men did not touch married women. What people did in their bedrooms did not bother Greek and Roman gods either.

Jewish Ethics

The usual Greek and Roman manner of life was a problem for the Jewish communities that had lived among Gentiles for centuries. It was undoubtedly easier to preserve Jewish ethics in almost purely Jewish villages in Palestine, where social control was certainly strong. But Gentiles also lived in Palestine, and Greek influence was inevitable. The problems were strongest in big cities, like Alexandria in Egypt, where Jews lived in close contact with Greeks and part of the Jewish elite even received education like Greek youth. Assimilation was a danger. So what were they to do if young men heard the call of the big world?

As mentioned, some recent scholars claim that the Jewish manner of life did not deviate from how their neighbors lived. Although we admittedly know very little of the life of the Jewish masses, we know what their teachers taught. A fact all too seldom mentioned is that the first models for later Christian catechisms were written among the Jews of Jesus' times and precisely in Egypt. Unfortunately, none of them have been entirely preserved to us, but the almost word-for-word quotations in Jewish and Christian works help us understand their content. The only way to avoid assimilation was a continuous instruction in clear terms, and the catechisms were one method, although not the only method used.

A fixed element in the Jewish moral handbooks was instruction in sexual morals. Josephus used common tradition when summarizing the Torah (*Against Apion*, 2.199–203). He clearly says that a Jewish husband has sex only with his wife and that everything else is godless. An unknown Jew who wrote in Greek hexameter and pretended to be Phocylides, the famous Greek poet of the past, joined the tradition. He condemned premarital sex with strong words, saying that the bride must be locked inside until the wedding (Pseudo-Phocylides, v. 215). Philo, the great Alexandrian scholar, wrote a minor work on the Decalogue and a more extensive one on all of these commands. He rejects premarital sex with clear words.

We only have fragments of what Jewish teachers preached in the synagogue. But if we accurately study all the early Jewish works we have, we start to recognize common traditions. When the writers retold biblical accounts, they did not repeat them word for word. They were retold vividly, and the stories were enlarged or abbreviated, with explanations and clear "modernizations"—exactly as people today are used to doing in Sunday School. Some of these accounts show how Scripture was used to teach Jewish sexual morals.

A Lesson from Joseph

A good example of this is the account of how Joseph was sold into slavery in Potiphar's house. Mrs. Potiphar saw the young man and started to molest him with her proposals (Genesis 39). This account was a treasure for Jewish preachers, and we have several retold versions of it. Philo used it to tell how a young Jewish man must live, and he added a long speech by Joseph to the woman. He here describes the Jewish sexual morals as follows:

> What are you forcing me to? We children of the Hebrews follow laws and customs which are especially our own. Other nations are permitted after the fourteenth year to deal without interference with harlots and strumpets and all those who make a traffic of their bodies, but with us a courtesan is not even permitted to live, and death is the penalty appointed for women who ply this trade. Before the lawful union we know no mating with other women, but come as virgin men to virgin maidens. The end we seek in wedlock is not pleasure but begetting of lawful children. To this day I have remained pure, and I will not take the first step in transgression by committing adultery. (*De Iosepho*, 42–44)

Philo describes the manner of Greeks and Romans exactly as we encounter it in our sources. Greeks did not ban their young men from premarital sex, but Philo claims that Jews had other standards, and he makes Joseph an example of this. Neither the bride nor the bridegroom had sex before their wedding. The walls of Potiphar's house saw, according to Philo, the collision between two different sexual morals. We, of course, realize that he was especially worried about the collision centuries after Joseph, in Alexandria during his own time.

Philo was not the only one to use the events in Potiphar's house to teach Jewish sexual morals. Josephus also retells the account and makes Joseph say that he had, until this moment, not laid with a woman, and the first one was not to be the wife of his master (*Antiquities*, 2.40–59). The *Testament of Joseph* also retells the problems of Joseph, possibly reflecting on the problems Jewish slaves had during the time of the writer (2–9).

The Prayer of Tobias

The book of Tobit tells how Tobias married his wife and added a beautiful prayer when the doors were closed (8:4–8):

> When the door was shut and the two were alone, Tobias got up from the bed and said, "Sister, get up, and let us pray that the Lord may have mercy upon us." And Tobias began to pray, "Blessed art Thou, O God of our fathers, and blessed be Thy holy and glorious name for ever. Let the heavens and all Thy creatures bless Thee. Thou madest Adam and gavest him Eve his wife as a helper and support. From them the race of mankind has sprung. Thou didst say, 'It is not good that the man should be alone; let Us make a helper for him like himself.' And now, O Lord, I am not taking this sister of mine because of lust, but with sincerity. Grant that I may find mercy and may grow old together with her." And she said with him, "Amen." Then they both went to sleep for the night.

Jesus' Teachings

The morals Jewish teachers preached were clear, but this was, of course, not the entire truth about early Jewish life. Josephus, for example, bans the marriages of harlots and says that the offerings at their wedding were not accepted

(*Antiquities*, 4.25). This is only one example confirming that harlots did exist in his time and, as the New Testament also shows, they did not call men in vain.

Jesus also followed the Jewish tradition, as He did so often. He quotes what we call the Sixth Commandment and then goes on:

> You have heard that it was said, "You shall not commit adultery." But I say to you that everyone who looks at a woman with lustful intent has already committed adultery with her in his heart. If your right eye causes you to sin, tear it out and throw it away. For it is better that you lose one of your members than that your whole body be thrown into hell. And if your right hand causes you to sin, cut it off and throw it away. For it is better that you lose one of your members than that your whole body go into hell. (Matthew 5:27–30)

The translation correctly speaks of "adultery" because the words are a direct quotation from the Decalogue. Nevertheless, Jesus does not speak exclusively about a sex act. Here, as so often, the actual deed, in this case the sex act, is only the last link in a long chain that starts from the heart. To covet a woman means to entertain lustful desires that offend her right to walk down the street without being viewed as a sex object.

The Apostles' Teachings

Knowing the typical Greek and Roman manner of life especially helps us understand Paul's first letter to the Corinthians. When he wrote his letter, no one in Corinth had been a Christian for more than five years, because Paul arrived in Corinth in AD 49 and wrote the letter in about

AD 53. The Jewish Christians in Corinth had learned sexual morals similar to those Paul taught. But to the contrary, the Gentile Christian men had learned the loose sexual morals described above. The new religion required a new manner of life, so it is no wonder the sparks were flying. Paul speaks in the fifth chapter of a man who had not realized that something should have changed:

> It is actually reported that there is sexual immorality (πορνεία, *porneia*) among you, and of a kind that is not tolerated even among pagans, for a man has his father's wife. And you are arrogant! Ought you not rather to mourn? Let him who has done this be removed from among you. (vv. 1–2)

Paul does not hesitate to command that the church must "deliver this man to Satan" (v. 5), which shows how strict the discipline was in the early Christian churches. In the sixth chapter, he lays out the basics, showing how the common Greek manner of life differed from Christian sexual morals:

> Or do you not know that the unrighteous will not inherit the kingdom of God? Do not be deceived: neither the sexually immoral, nor idolaters, nor adulterers, nor men who practice homosexuality, nor thieves, nor the greedy, nor drunkards, nor revilers, nor swindlers will inherit the kingdom of God. And such were some of you. But you were washed, you were sanctified, you were justified in the name of the Lord Jesus Christ and by the Spirit of our God.

> "All things are lawful for me," but not all things are helpful. "All things are lawful for me," but I will not be dominated by anything. "Food is meant for the stomach and the stomach for food"—and God will destroy both one and the other. The body is not meant for sexual immorality (τῇ πορνείᾳ, *te porneia*), but for the Lord, and the Lord for the body. And God raised the Lord and will also raise us up by His power. Do you not know that your bodies are members of Christ? Shall I then take the members of Christ and make them members of a prostitute? Never! Or do you not know that he who is joined to a prostitute becomes one body with her? For, as it is written, "The two will become one flesh." But he who is joined to the Lord becomes one spirit with Him. Flee from sexual immorality (τὴν πορνείαν, *tēn porneian*). Every other sin a person commits is outside the body, but the sexually immoral person (ὁ δὲ πορνεύων, *ho de porneuon*) sins against his own body. Or do you not know that your body is a temple of the Holy Spirit within you, whom you have from God? You are not your own, for you were bought with a price. So glorify God in your body. (vv. 9–20)

We should note the words Paul uses here. Μοιχεία, *moicheia*, and words from this stem denote adultery, in other words, sex with the wife or husband of another person. The sense of πορνεία, *porneia*, is wider and undoubtedly here means other kinds of relations, in other words, all sex before or outside of marriage. Paul here thus accurately follows the Jewish morals as we know them.

It is easy to understand life in the young church of Corinth. The practices in Gentile Corinth greatly differed from what Paul and other Christian teachers taught and expected from the converts. The Corinthians had to learn a new lifestyle. They did, but they also returned to old manners, sinned, and tried to repent and start over again.

Some of the wandering teachers seem to have been rather like predators, seeking the favor of "weak women" (2 Timothy 3:6) and behaving in banquets as Gentile men used to act:

> They have eyes full of adultery, insatiable for sin. They entice unsteady souls. They have hearts trained in greed. Accursed children! (2 Peter 2:14)

The author of Hebrews, anonymous to us, only briefly writes about marriage:

> Let marriage be held in honor among all, and let the marriage bed be undefiled, for God will judge the sexually immoral (πόρνους, *pornous*) and adulterous (μοιχούς, *moichous*). (Hebrews 13:4)

Early Christian Teachings

It should now be easy to understand what the letter says: God will judge the "adulterer" and the "sexually immoral." The author tells both married and unmarried people to follow the instruction given to them. The message is as clear as it is in the Pauline Epistles and still clearer where Christian teachers directly copied Jewish moral handbooks, as in the *Epistle of Barnabas* and in the *Didache*:

> You shall not be sexually promiscuous; you shall not commit adultery; you shall not corrupt children (παιδοφθορήσεις, *paidophthorēseis*). (*Epistle of Barnabas* 19:4)

> You shall not murder; you shall not commit adultery; you shall not corrupt children (παιδοφθορήσεις, *paidophthorēseis*); you shall not be sexually immoral. (*Didache* 2:2)

Jewish people in Jesus' time had learned to live as a minority, and this was something the first Gentile Christians also had to learn. It was never easy, and Christian teachers had to repeatedly use strong words witnessing the continuous fight between the old and the new manner of life in the hearts of converts.

Slaves

Slaves who became Christians had an equally difficult time. A slave belonged to his owner as property. Petronius (d. AD 66) tells in his satire of the house of the newly rich Trimalchio, and also of his ugly and fat pet boy, called Croesus (*Trimalchio*, 64). Many slaves might have appreciated the attention of their master, and Josephus makes Mrs. Potiphar greatly wonder why Joseph did not do what she expected him to do (*Antiquities*, 2.40). But what happened if the master did not leave even a dog alone, as Petronius tells about an old man (*Trimalchio*, 43), but the Christian instruction given to a slave says not to share the bed with him? Some sources seem to tell what it meant. An anonymous writer describing in detail the problems of Joseph with Mrs. Potiphar may give a model to his fellow Jews: It was better to be beaten in prison than to fulfill the hopes of the lady or master (*Testament of Joseph*).

Christian teachers recognized the problems. Hippolytus made men who asked for Baptism either marry their concubines or end the relationships. He also admitted the female slaves living in concubinage to Baptism, provided that they had raised the children of their master and that there were no other men in their lives. We only ask what the recipients of 1 Peter, for example, had suffered in the houses in which they served.

Reflection Questions

- Try to imagine yourself living the life of a young girl or boy in an ancient Greek or Roman town. Describe what would be different from your childhood and what would be similar.

- Greek and Roman morals allowed young boys to have numerous sexual affairs, but girls were not allowed to. What was the moral code for boys and girls when you grew up? Does our world's moral code allow numerous sexual affairs to both genders equally? From your interactions with friends, coworkers, and others who exploit this sexual freedom, do you think it really makes people happier?

- Try to imagine yourself as a Jewish or Christian slave girl or boy, where you are considered your master's sexual property. How would you try to honor Christ?

4

Men and Men, Women and Women

When it comes to same-sex affairs, secular culture has drastically changed in just a few decades. This has challenged traditional Christian ethics. Yet, as they say, there is nothing new under the sun. In fact, the challenges Christians face today would have been very familiar to the first Christians.

Greek Views of Homosexuality

The Greek world of antiquity was heterogeneous. However, when it came to same-sex affairs, all signs pointed to the same ways of thinking. Modern writers often claim that in the ancient world, the only kind of homosexuality people were familiar with was aggressive and based on sex, not love. But this is not true. In the famous *Symposium* by Plato, you easily see the ideas of Athenian nobility in the classical period. For them, bisexual behavior was known already by the age at which—expressed in our terms—sexual orientation was formed, and same-sex affairs were common. In Plato's dialogue, Aristophanes the comic poet tells us a comical tale of the origin of the sexes, which nicely illustrates this point. According to his tale, in the beginning of humanity, there were three genders: male, female, and androgynous. Each person had four hands, four legs, two heads and two sets of genitals. The gods, however, sliced each person in two, with the result being that everyone desperately seeks their other half in order to reconnect with it. If the lost half of a man were feminine, he loves women, but if it were masculine, he seeks love from men. Similarly, Plato mentions women seeking women. But even though men who loved men married women, they only did so to acquire offspring because the law said legitimate children could only be conceived between a married man and woman.

Of course, only a fool takes Plato's Aristophanes seriously. More important is what Plato then makes Socrates say in the dialogue. Socrates presents how men should deal with the boys they love. According to Socrates, selfish people find new targets and do not hesitate to abandon the boy they had previously loved. In contrast, good men remain faithful to their beloved and appreciate not only their beauty. In this way, Plato's *Symposium* opens to us an important window, showing that educated Hellenistic Jews and Christians were aware of more than just the modern caricature of ancient aggressive homosexuality. This kind of homosexual relationship included a strong bond based on friendship, and that was, according to Plato, the reason why Ionians, for example, rejected homoeroticism. Numerous tyrants had lost their lives after the lover had avenged what had happened to his partner.

Pederasty

Accordingly, there should be an important distinction made between pederasty (a grown-up man who loved a young boy) and sex between adults. The Greek tradition was familiar with both. For instance, Homer's *The Iliad* includes the story of love between Achilles and Patroclus, who were both adults; tradition could not decide who was older. It seems that of these two models, pederasty was by far the more common. In Sparta, homosexuality was institutional. At least in some societies, pederasty was seen as a continuum: A young boy was at first the object of an older man, and when he grew up, he took a young boy for himself. In Athens, this continuum assumed important pedagogical elements. Plato, with his sense of humor, presents how Charmides, the most beautiful of Athenian boys, entered a palaestra (wrestling school) and the crowd, including Socrates, welcomed him like Miss World today (*Charmides*).

A speech written by Lysias (*Peri traumatos*) tells a less beautiful story from Athens in the classical period. Two men had loved a boy, and both sought his favor. The mutual hate between the older lovers escalated and spurred one of them to invade the home of the other, even into the women's quarters, which were forbidden to men. There he encountered his rival's wife and daughters, who usually never saw men. Evidently, for Lysias, it was not at all unusual that a man who had a wife at home would still pursue a homoerotic affair with a boy, though this is not the point Lysias was making. This reflected common values: A wife was there to deliver legal offspring, and the real, passionate love life was found outside the house, in homosexual relations.

This landscape hardly changed in the Hellenistic period, which followed the classical period. Roman historian Cornelius Nepos describes the Cretan ideal for men as having been loved by as many men as possible in the preface of his work. Homoerotic relations continued to be very common in the Greek world. This caused peculiar problems for modern Christians who taught classical and Hellenistic texts at schools. Not all the books on the shelves were meant to be read by the young pupils. For instance, when translating Theocritus's Greek verses (third century BC) into English, translators at times abandoned English and used Latin instead in the sections they viewed as salacious. Or they simply omitted those parts in order to protect young pupils from reading them.

Sex Between Women

In contrast with men, sex between women does not appear very often in the sources we have. This is not unexpected, as the vast majority of remaining texts were written by men, and they predominantly reflect male society. As mentioned, Plato briefly refers to relations between women in *Symposium*, and sources allude to an apparently widespread practice in ancient Sparta. The touching verses of Sappho (seventh–sixth century BC), the great poetess of Lesbos, are an important exception. We have only fragments of her songs, and few if any of her texts are complete. Her songs, along with her role with the young girls she seems to have been associated with, have been understood in wildly different ways in the centuries that have passed. In her most famous poem, she wonders how an unnamed man is able to sit near a beautiful woman and behave normally, while a mere look at the woman makes the poetess totally confused. Modern commentators on the poem reflect the history of Western sexual ideals. Is it simply a love poem, reflecting on lesbian love between women? Or is the poetess a matriarch, teaching young girls the secrets of heterosexual love? Various interpretations clearly show the ideals and fears of the interpreters themselves. However, from this song and others, it seems clear that Sappho's work reflects something at least rather close to what we are more familiar with on the male side of history.

Homosexuality in Rome

In Rome, the ethics were a little different from those in the Greek culture. The old Roman tradition did not appreciate open homoeroticism. At least in the early times, it was seen as something alien to Roman culture. Plautus the comic poet (third–second century BC) still refers to it as *pergraecari*, in other words, "live like the Greeks." Catullus (early first century BC) tells about his unpleasant experiences during his military service under a commander who misused him and whom he nicknamed *Mentula*, which is better left untranslated here. The ethics were changing, however, as is seen in the golden age of Roman literature. Virgil (first century BC) reshapes the idyll of Theocritus, with its homoerotic colors, and his contemporary Horace does not hesitate to tell how he takes a slave boy when needed (*Epistles*, 1.2:31–35). Petronius (first century AD) tells in his satire, mentioned above, how Trimalchio, now a rich man, had a pet boy as a sex object. It is important to note that these texts do not reflect the pedagogical love affair we saw in the Athens of Plato's time. Instead, they mostly allude to affairs based on the satisfaction of the sexual desires of the stronger partner. As we saw with Catullus, it was not a particular honor or an enlightening pedagogical experience for him to serve as a sex object. Nevertheless, bisexuality, understood here as having sexual relations with both sexes, was a conventional part of sexual ethics during the first centuries AD.

Jewish Views of Homosexuality

The Old Testament clearly rejects sex between men and seems not to leave room for different interpretations. The Mosaic Law seems to be clear enough:

> You shall not lie with a male as with a woman; it is an abomination. (Leviticus 18:22)
>
> If a man lies with a male as with a woman, both of them have committed an abomination; they shall surely be put to death; their blood is upon them." (Leviticus 20:13)

Scholars consider these verses to be a part of the Holiness Code (Leviticus 17–26) and put them in the context of other sexual offenses. The word "abomination" (*to'eba*) is often linked to idolatry, and that is why some interpreters have tried to limit the command only to homoerotic affairs in context with foreign cults. But in general, *to'eba* does not only refer to idolatry but has a much wider sense. The Holiness Code also rejects incest and marriages between close relatives, and this seems to have nothing to do with idolatry. Moreover, the rulings are older than the current form of the Holiness Code, and early Jewish teachers had taken them as they had apparently been before the Holiness Code: a general rejection of sex between males.

Jewish writers known to us follow this line strictly. Josephus briefly presents the Jewish manner of life to his Gentile readers (*Apion*, 2.199–203). He adds a strict rejection of sex between males:

> [The Law] abhorred male intercourse with males, and the penalty is death if anyone were to attempt such. (*Apion*, 2.199)

This kind of rejection seems to have been a standing element of Jewish moral handbooks. Pseudo-Phocylides, mentioned above, does not seek beautiful words:

> Do not transgress with unlawful sex the limits set by nature. For even animals are not pleased by intercourse of male with male. And let women not imitate the sexual role of men. (190–92)

Philo, who lived in Greek Egypt, deals with the question often, and finds strong words too (e.g., *On the Special Laws*, 3:37–42; *Abr.*, 136; *Contempl.*, 62). This time, Philo stood at a crossroads. He greatly appreciated Plato, whose ideas usually meant knowledge to him, not opinions. Here he has to choose between two masters, and he does not hesitate to follow Moses and abandon Plato.

Jewish writers known to us thus clearly followed the Torah. We should also be careful here not to underestimate the diversity of early Judaism. Jewish cosmopolites who assimilated with Greek ideals funded Olympic Games, ordained theater, and even built Gentile shrines in cities they governed. No wonder that Herod, according to Josephus (*Antiquities*, 16.229–32), admired beautiful eunuchs at his court. He hardly asked for ethical instruction from Jewish teachers of the Law, and he was not the only one of his sort.

New Testament Writings on Homosexuality

The most important New Testament passage addressing sex between males is in Romans 1:24–28. In the wider context, Paul is presenting Gentiles as sinners, not as individuals but collectively. They look at God's creation, but they have refused to serve the Creator. They have "exchanged the glory of the immortal God for images resembling mortal man and birds and animals and creeping things" (v. 23). They have abandoned God, and God has abandoned them to live in sin.

Paul uses sex between males as an example of how far they have gone from God:

> For this reason God gave them up to dishonorable passions. For their women exchanged natural relations for those that are contrary to nature; and the men likewise gave up natural relations with women and were consumed with passion for one another, men committing shameless acts with men and receiving in themselves the due penalty for their error. (vv. 26–27)

Paul thus links same-sex affairs and idolatry into his big picture: Humanity has abandoned God to serve idols; subsequently, God has abandoned humanity to live in its various sins. He first mentions same-sex affairs, but then he adds a long list of sins at the end of the chapter. Abandoning God has led men to homoeroticism, but also to a lack of love, to murder, and to revolt against their parents. The missing contact with God has led men to sin, and to Paul, homoeroticism was an example of this. It certainly was received well among his Jewish readers. Greeks rejected the scriptural teaching—they were proud of their wisdom—and now were confronted with the fact that a kind of love they greatly appreciated was punishable by death in the Torah.

Sex between men often appears in early Christian lists of sins:

> Or do you not know that the unrighteous will not inherit the kingdom of God? Do not be deceived: neither the sexually immoral, nor idolaters, nor adulterers, nor men who practice homosexuality, nor thieves, nor the greedy, nor drunkards, nor revilers, nor swindlers

> will inherit the kingdom of God. And such were some of you. But you were washed, you were sanctified, you were justified in the name of the Lord Jesus Christ and by the Spirit of our God. (1 Corinthians 6:9–11)

The Greek text in verse 9 distinguishes between persons who are ἀρσενοκοῖται, *arsenokoitai*, probably the active person in the act, and μαλακοί, *malakoi*, probably the passive person in the act. The ESV, like many other translations, has abandoned this distinction and only speaks of "men who practice homosexuality." They, as many other kinds of men, are included in those who will not inherit the kingdom of God. The introductory words "or do you not know" show that everyone should know the moral instruction, probably because the list of sins was taught at the moment of Baptism often mentioned in similar passages. The early church thus ensured that new Christians knew what the new path they had found expected from them.

Another passage is in 1 Timothy:

> Understanding this, that the law is not laid down for the just but for the lawless and disobedient, for the ungodly and sinners, for the unholy and profane, for those who strike their fathers and mothers, for murderers, the sexually immoral, men who practice homosexuality, enslavers, liars, perjurers, and whatever else is contrary to sound doctrine. (1:9–10)

Early Christian Writings

Early Christian writings follow this path. Polycarp, the bishop of Smyrna, directly quotes 1 Corinthians in his letter to the Philippians (5:3). The *Epistle of Barnabas* and the *Didache* also here quote a Jewish moral handbook word for word:

> You shall not be sexually promiscuous; you shall not commit adultery; you shall not corrupt children (παιδοφθορήσεις, *paidophthorēseis*). (*Epistle of Barnabas* 19:4)
>
> You shall not murder; you shall not commit adultery; you shall not corrupt children (παιδοφθορήσεις, *paidophthorēseis*); you shall not be sexually immoral. (*Didache* 2:2)

παιδοφθορήσεις, *paidophthorēseis*, is here translated "to corrupt children" (M. Holmes). But often, "you shall not commit pederasty" undoubtedly refers to pederasty. These quotations make it clear how Christian teachers unanimously went on fighting for the Christian manner of life as they had been taught.

The Effect of Jewish and Christian Morals

Early Jewish and Christian morals clearly deviated from the conventional Greek and Roman manner of life by condemning same-sex relations and bisexuality. The minority religion grew stronger over the centuries, and Europe became a Christian continent. This does not mean that old habits disappeared. Nevertheless, the new conventional instruction proclaimed that it was a sin to live in same-sex relations and widely wiped it from public life. It took more than a thousand years before the big turn arrived after World War II. Since then, all Christian churches have lost much of their strength. The Western churches have either finally found the true Gospel, or, as I think, they have started to compromise with the morals of the majority in their environment, which also have grown to be the majority of their members. This has caused tensions between conservative and liberal members of the churches, but it has also caused tensions between Christians in the West and in the developing countries. Everyone who still remembers the atmosphere shortly after WWII from his own experience can only marvel at how rapidly conventional morals have changed. It is certainly useful to look back at the earliest history of the church to see how early Christians dealt with their social environment.

Reflection Questions

- A good rule is that Christians should read two books: the Bible and God's creation. In other words, listen to the Word of God and understand that the Scriptures accord well with good order in the created world. Are you able to read both books here? How can doing so help Christians speak to people who live contrary to God's design for life?

- The view on homoeroticism has changed in the Western world, first by the effects of Christian mission making it morally unacceptable, and then by rapidly bringing back its acceptability again during the last half century. Why did that happen? How does it influence our societies?

- How much attention should Christians give to trying to influence the laws of their countries? How much attention should they give to instructing their own people?

5

Family People in Corinth or Galilean Eunuchs for the Sake of the Kingdom: Marriage or Single Life?

The early church followed its Jewish mother religion in most moral questions. As a result, it differed from the conventional manner of life among the Greeks and Romans. Some ideals, however, set Christians apart from both Jews and Gentiles. Already, the New Testament greatly honored single life, an attitude foreign to mainline Judaism. After the New Testament era, single life came to be considered significantly better than marriage, which is where the early church also deviated from its own holy writings.

Greek and Roman Views of Marriage

Greeks and Romans married so their children would be legitimate citizens in the eyes of society. Children were expected to take care of their aged parents. It was also considered a duty toward the city to marry and produce free citizens. Nevertheless, both the Greek cities and later Rome itself suffered from producing too few children.

Since sex was easily available for men, they were often not eager to marry and raise children. Greek philosophers sometimes expressed their dislike of conventional family life. Seneca the Stoic refers to Theophrastus, the famous Peripatetic philosopher, who rejected all of the traditional reasons for marriage: to raise children, to preserve one's name, to be cared for in old age, or to get heirs. Officials were worried because all too many young men preferred single life. Plautus the comic makes an old man praise his freedom:

> Since I have many relations, what need have I of children? Now I live well and happily, and as I like, and as contents my feelings. For I shall bequeath my property to my relations, and divide it among them. These, like children, pay attention to me; they come to see how I do, or what I want; before it is daybreak they are with me; they make inquiry how I have enjoyed my sleep in the night. (*Miles Gloriosus*, 705–8)

Authorities did not appreciate single life, but it would have been the choice of many young men, especially in Imperial Rome. They were often reminded of their duties toward their society. Metellus Numidicus, a Roman consul, wrote as follows:

> If we could get on without a wife, Romans, we would all avoid that annoyance; but since nature has ordained that we can neither live very comfortably with them nor at all without them, we must take thought for our lasting well-being rather than for the pleasure of the moment. (Cornelius Gellius, *Attic Nights*, Book 1, 6:1–2)

Caesar Augustus also emphasized the duties of a citizen (Suetonius, *Octavianus*, 89; Livius, *Epitome*, 59) and, like many others, he did not even try to argue that marriage would lead to happiness. It was reason and the good of the city that should lead young men to marry. The Spartan state supported these arguments with rewards and punishments (Aristoteles, *De re publica*, 2.6:3), and citizens were required by law to marry also in Athens (Plato, *Symposium* 192b). In Rome, censors fined young men who delayed their marriage too long (Cicero, *De legibus*, 3.3:7). Augustus's reforms after the bloody civil wars favored families that had at least three children. Marriage and children could also boost the careers of officials. It appears that a single man did not inherit anything, and childless men received only half of the due inheritance. These examples show that the emperors did not hesitate, on occasion, to enter an area usually reserved for individual choice. They also hint at a common problem throughout the Mediterranean world—there were too few children.

Marriage was thus a very strong institution in the Greek and Roman worlds, although in many ways different from modern ideas. Authorities tried to defend and support it. They certainly thought that family and marriage were the nucleus of society.

Jewish Views of Marriage

Younger generations took care of their elderly relatives in Israel as well, and it meant that marriage was also greatly appreciated among the Hebrews. People needed offspring to secure their old age. Many old texts show how people wished that the nation would grow (e.g., Ruth 4:11; Jeremiah 29:6). It was a shame to be childless, as was Abraham and Sarah's lot for a long time, as well as later Hannah, the mother of Samuel (Genesis 12–21; 1 Samuel 1). The book of Ruth and several psalms also show that home, family, and children were what people longed for.

However, an abstract appreciation of marriage and children was not enough for mainstream early Judaism. God had told the first humans to "be fruitful and multiply" (Genesis 1:28). Many teachers considered this a command, not a mere blessing. Everyone had to marry and procreate to fulfill the command. The harshest interpretations declared that a marriage that was childless after a certain time should be annulled. To be childless was a shame to Philo (*Questions and Answers on Exodus 2:19*), and if a man continued on in marriage with a fruitless woman, it showed that he only sought pleasure (*On the Special Laws*, 3:34–36). He did not accept that a man would marry a woman older than he was (*Questions and Answers on Genesis 1:27*).

What Philo says seems to have been a common opinion in early Judaism. We meet similar views in early rabbinic collections, in the Mishna and Tosefta. According to the Mishna, a wife being "fruitless" was a legitimate reason for divorce (Mishna, *Gittin* 4:8), and the Tosefta bans marriage if the woman is fruitless or older than the man (Tosefta, *Yebamot* 8:4). It is easy to understand that single life was not approved of in this kind of world. To be true, there were a few exceptions: Some philosophers admired Jewish groups that rejected marriage, and a part of the Essenes—a mystic sect dedicated to austere ideals—banned sex, which was considered unclean. Nevertheless, mainline Judaism considered marriage both a blessing and a duty. And as we will discuss in chapter 7, marriage also required procreation.

Jesus' Views of Marriage and Single Life

What Jesus taught about single life was an exception in this context. He rejected divorce and remarriage (see chapters 9 and 10), and when His disciples were rather stunned by that, He added something that might have added to their surprise:

> The disciples said to Him, "If such is the case of a man with his wife, it is better not to marry." But He said to them, "Not everyone can receive this saying, but only those to whom it is given. For there are eunuchs who have been so from birth, and there are eunuchs who have been made eunuchs by men, and there are eunuchs who have made themselves eunuchs for the sake of the kingdom of heaven. Let the one who is able to receive this receive it." (Matthew 19:10–12)

The sense of the word εὐνοῦχοι, *eunouchoi* (eunuchs), is clear, and it is probably a translation of the Aramaic *srysym*. The opponents had apparently mocked Jesus and His disciples as eunuchs because they used to walk around together and had abandoned the duty to procreate. Jesus said that marriage was not meant for everyone, and He listed three reasons for abandoning marriage. There are people who, from birth, are physically unable to marry. These kinds of people are often mentioned in the Mishna and Tosefta. There are also people who were eunuchs because they had been castrated, but it was also possible to be a eunuch "for the sake of the kingdom of heaven."

The insult was thus turned around. To be single may be a deliberate choice of an individual. It does not imply that a person has turned his back on God's commands, but, on the contrary, it reflects a deep commitment to the kingdom of heaven. This had led the disciples to leave everything and follow Jesus. They had not overlooked God's command, but they had followed it, and they would be richly rewarded because of it (Matthew 19:27–30). Single life is here presented in an extraordinarily favorable light, which was not usual in early Judaism.

THE APOSTLES' TEACHINGS AND THE EARLY CHURCH

Paul addresses marriage in 1 Corinthians 7, a chapter that should never be overlooked when discussing Christian marriage. Paul here greatly appreciates single life as a role given by God. He does not show a clear preference for marriage or for single life, but He warns of persecutions that were about to come soon. It is not easy for a modern reader to determine which of the two paths would please God more. Paul also says that to be single can be a "gift," meaning that a single person is happy in her or his life and takes it as a mission given by God.

Paul might have been ambivalent when speaking about marriage and single life, but most early church fathers did not hide their preferences. Their models were the apostles, who left everything and followed Jesus, and they appreciated virginity more than marriage (cf. 1 Corinthians 9:5). Unlike in early Judaism, marriage and procreation were never regarded as a duty in early Christianity. Marriage was rather allowed for people who could not live according to the higher standards. According to Tertullian, marriage is good, but abstinence is better:

> What, however, is better than this "good," we learn from the apostle, who permits marrying indeed, but prefers abstinence; the former on account of the insidiousness of temptations, the latter on account of the straits of the times. Now, by looking into the reason thus given for each proposition, it is easily discerned that the ground on which the power of marrying is conceded is necessity; but whatever necessity grants, she by her very nature depreciates. In fact, in that it is written, "To marry is better than to burn," what, pray, is the nature of this "good" which is (only) commended by comparison with "evil," so that the reason why "marrying" is more good is (merely) that "burning" is less? Nay, but how far better is it neither to marry nor to burn? (*To His Wife*, 1:3)

Tertullian does not just present a strange opinion here, but it would be easy to quote dozens of passages from the early church fathers strongly preferring virginity to marriage. To be true, Jerome (ca. AD 347–420) said that there was no reason to vilify silver [marriage], although gold [virginity] is more precious (*Adversus Jovinianum*, 1:3). Marriage was, however, mostly defended in a modest manner, and some church fathers did not defend it at all. Jerome considered every sexual union unclean (*Adversus Jovinianum*, 1:20). Methodius, who was apparently martyred in AD 311, reshapes Plato's famous *Symposium*, letting women discuss holiness, not love. They strongly prefer virginity to marriage: The holy history advances from polygamy to monogamy and subsequently to virginity.

Virginity was thus greatly appreciated, but how strongly was this "gold" preferred to "silver"? Some teachers, for example Marcion (ca. AD 85–160), Tatian (d. ca. AD 185), and several Gnostic sects, had labeled marriage a sin, but this was never mainstream in early Christianity. Clement of Alexandria strongly rejected those views, calling marriage holy (*Stromateis*, 3.12:84) and recommending it by arguing that a couple acted together with the Creator (*Paedagogus*, 2.10:83). The Synod in Gangra (AD 340) condemned people who labeled marriage as a sin:

> If any one shall condemn marriage, or abominate and condemn a woman who is a believer and devout, and sleeps with her own husband, as though she could not enter the Kingdom [of heaven] let him be anathema. (Canon 1)

The strong words simultaneously show that opposite opinions appeared within the church. Ordinary Christians might also defend their manner of life with a strong hand. Jerome had, according to rumors, called marriage a sin in Rome. Stones started to fly, and the famous teacher had to leave the city.

PREFERENCE FOR SINGLE LIFE

Many church fathers thus clearly preferred single life to marriage. Like many of them, Tertullian struggled to have a consistent line here. On the one hand, he says that coveting always precedes marriage (*On Exhortation to Chastity*, 9), and as seen, he strongly prefers abstinence to marriage. On the other hand, however, he praises marriage between two Christians so eloquently that it merits an extensive quote:

> Whence are we to find (words) enough fully to tell the happiness of that marriage which the church cements, and the oblation confirms, and the benediction signs and seals; (which) angels carry back the news of (to heaven), (which) the Father holds for ratified? For even on earth children do not rightly and lawfully wed without their fathers' consent. What kind of yoke is that of two believers, (partakers) of one hope, one desire, one discipline, one and the same service? Both (are) brethren, both fellow servants, no difference of spirit or of flesh; nay, (they are) truly two in one flesh. Where the flesh is one, one is the spirit too. Together they pray, together prostrate themselves, together perform their fasts; mutually teaching, mutually exhorting, mutually sustaining. Equally (are they) both (found) in the church of God; equally at the banquet of God; equally in straits, in persecutions, in refreshments. Neither hides (ought) from the other; neither shuns the other; neither is troublesome to the other. The sick is visited, the indigent relieved, with freedom. Alms (are given) without (danger of ensuing) torment; sacrifices (attended) without scruple; daily diligence (discharged) without impediment: (there is) no stealthy signing, no trembling greeting, no mute benediction. Between the two echo psalms and hymns; and they mutually challenge each other which shall better chant to their Lord. Such things when Christ sees and hears, He joys. To these He sends His own peace. Where two (are), there

> withal (is) He Himself. Where He (is), there the Evil One is not. (*To His Wife*, 2:8)

Nevertheless, marriage was never considered a duty like it was in mainstream Judaism. So why did the early church so rapidly and so radically abandon its own heritage? Jesus praised marriage, and 1 Timothy 4:1–5 strongly warns of teachers banning marriage:

> Now the Spirit expressly says that in later times some will depart from the faith by devoting themselves to deceitful spirits and teachings of demons, through the insincerity of liars whose consciences are seared, who forbid marriage and require abstinence from foods that God created to be received with thanksgiving by those who believe and know the truth. For everything created by God is good, and nothing is to be rejected if it is received with thanksgiving, for it is made holy by the word of God and prayer.

Early Christians forgot or overlooked these warnings for several reasons. The church fathers mostly did not identify themselves with ordinary Christians living family lives in Corinth, but rather with the "eunuchs for the sake of the kingdom of heaven" (Matthew 19:12), Galilean fishermen who left their nets and families, and even those who hated their wives (Luke 14:26) in order to follow Jesus without compromise. Ascetic ideals and monasteries signified a wholehearted commitment to God, and Christian writers could also expect that their disciplinary manner of life was generally accepted and honored. Early Jewish teachers already proclaimed that the goal of marital sex was to conceive children and not to gain pleasure (see ch. 7). But ascetic ideals grew stronger overall in the Roman Imperial period. Neoplatonism in the early third century strongly distinguished between the body and soul, and everything connected with the body was less appreciated. Gentile philosophers followed strict diets and distinguished between eating and pleasure. As so often in the history of the church, Christians were inclined to follow current wisdom, and abstinence and virginity were compatible with it. It was possible to be a Christian and live in a family, but a serious commitment meant renouncing ordinary life and marriage. Slowly but clearly, a perception started to take hold that single Christians were better than married people.

A Mishandling of the Bible

It was not easy to find biblical support for these new ideas. God's words on marriage in Genesis 1 presented a problem, and so did the Old Testament heroes, like the patriarchs. Jesus had taught that single life is an option, and Paul might have appreciated this option even more. This was, however, not enough. Several church fathers strongly distinguished between the Old and New Testaments (Christians do not marry their sisters like the first men, and do not have several wives as the patriarchs) or interpreted everything allegorically (procreation means that people produce good ideas and deeds). Origen, at least, distinguished between those living in flesh and marrying, and those living in spirit and choosing virginity. This mishandling of Paul nestled into the Christian tradition during the next thousand years, and even Martin Luther, a strong critic of nonbiblical traditions, still followed this vein in his early Invocavit sermons in 1521. Augustine had considered marriage a concession and virginity a real ideal in 1 Corinthians 7 (the concession in reality being that a couple may refrain from sex for a mutually agreed time). The ideal of virginity later led to forced celibacy in the Western Church. Although most Mosaic commands were abandoned, teachers arbitrarily picked the rulings saying that sex made the couple unclean (Leviticus 15:16–18). The pastors of the New Testament were compared to Old Testament priests, the deacons to Levites, and the Sacraments to Old Testament sacrifices. Consequently, celibacy was regarded as a necessity, because a priest may suddenly encounter a person who needed to be baptized or to receive the Eucharist, and he was unclean if he had slept with his wife during the night. The first papal letters requiring celibacy were written about AD 400, and they clearly show that the role of the Scripture was to humbly support what was already decided with other arguments. Ascetic ideals and monasteries had long before rendered the option given by Jesus a much better one than marriage, and finally a duty for pastors. The Eastern Church never accepted forced celibacy, although it, too, greatly appreciated virginity. In the West, the ideal remained unchallenged until the Reformation challenged it along with so many other parts of church tradition.

Western Christianity thus drastically deviated from the teachings of Judaism. Jesus and Paul had appreciated single life and considered it a possible path given by God. But it was only after some centuries that single life was clearly preferred to marriage. The ascetic ideals had led people to look at God's creation, sexuality, and marriage from a new point of view.

Reflection Questions

- How welcome does an unmarried adult feel within your church? How can a church better serve its unmarried adults?

- What challenges do individuals who are involuntarily single face in our churches?

- What does Paul mean by his "own gift"; in other words, living a single life (1 Corinthians 7)?

6

What Is Marriage? How Was It Made?

Marriage is an institution known to almost every human society throughout history. Though there have been variations, the most common form of marriage has been a lifelong union between a single man and a single woman. But was this the case in the world of the first Christians?

For the Mediterranean world, the Hellenistic and early Roman Imperial periods (330 BC–AD 114) brought on a kind of globalization. Consolidating military and political power allowed these empires to increase travel and trade, which made the known world smaller and brought the sea of people around the Mediterranean Sea into closer contact with one another. Here, however, we reach the limits of our data. There was a great host of different cultures, languages, and tribes, and we simply do not know how all of these people used to practice marriage and how they used to live in their families. Some Greek and Roman writers were keen to tell tales of distant peoples, the intent of which was, in part, to amuse their readers with strange manners. The trustworthiness of such stories is rather suspect. We know more about traditional Greek and Roman practices, but we should understand that the apostles likely did not see the same sort of practices when traveling, for example, through the regions of modern-day Turkey.

As stated in previous chapters, in Greek and Roman societies, the main reason people got married was to conceive lawful children. It should also be clear now that faithfulness in marriage, as we understand it, was expected and demanded only of wives, not of men. For men, sexual relations were rarely limited to marriage, as it was not unusual or morally frowned upon for the husband to continue to have sex with slave girls and harlots after his wedding. He would also often have sex with males.

How Marriage Was Made in Greece

In Athens, a law in 451 BC decreed that only children born to married citizens of Athens could receive the rights of citizens. In effect, then, this law prevented marriages between the citizen upper class and the noncitizen lower class. It also closed the door to free Greeks in other cities. The reason for this restriction was simple: to preserve the power of the small upper echelon of Athens' citizens. For the most part, our sources tell us about the lives of these free citizens. A sentence in a speech wrongly attributed to the Athenian orator Demosthenes shows the marital values common to this class:

> Mistresses we keep for the sake of pleasure, concubines for the daily care of our persons, but wives to bear us legitimate children and to be faithful guardians of our households. (*Against Neaera*, 122)

Married life was very different in Sparta, where all of the male citizens were expected to devote their time to the military. Thus, few would be able to take care of their domestic affairs in the city. They mainly left their estates to the care of their wives, who, in this way, had an important role to play in society. In contrast, the place of the women of Athens was at home, and their role in society was very small. Even a girl born in a wealthy Athenian family grew up with few contacts outside of her house. As we saw, Cornelius Nepos wondered why Greeks—and not only Athenians—did not allow their housewives to eat with guests at their banquets. A housewife was expected to give birth to children, take care of the house, and stay in the background.

We do not know much about the actual marriage ceremony in the ancient Greek city-states. Greek writers in general assumed, with good reason, that people knew how marriages took place, and that is why they did not usually describe their customs. We have to collect small fragments, like a jigsaw puzzle, and we would like to know more. Again, we are most familiar with life in Athens in the classical period. There it was customary for parents to arrange their children's marriages early. The bride, who in most cases was under twenty years old—and in upper-class families hardly in her teens—spent her last days as a single woman in her father's house with her friends and performed important offerings. The wedding night was celebrated with a big crowd, with torches lighting the night.

Greek Marriage Contracts

Humans are clever in devising ways to protect their loved ones in need, and this certainly was the case when a family gave their young daughter to a bridegroom. The father did not want his daughter to be mishandled or humiliated by the husband, who was usually about thirty years old. After the marriage, however, the husband had considerable, almost limitless, power over his young wife in his own household, where her family could not easily protect her. So, what was there to do? A family could make sure their daughter would be protected with a marriage contract. The wife brought a dowry with her, and, at least in some cases, the sum of money may have been very significant. In Athens in the fifth century BC, Alcibiades got no fewer than ten talents from his father-in-law (Andocides, *Against Alcibiades*, 13–14). The husband could not freely use the money, as, depending on the contract, it was possible for the father-in-law to demand it back if the husband broke the contract agreement (see *Demosthenes*, 59:52). In this way, the marriage contract protected the wife from humiliation and misery. Also, it afforded the wife some protection in case her husband died. These contracts could be very specific. The Egyptian sand has preserved such contracts for us. This one was written in 311 BC and found in Elephantine:

> In the seventh year of the reign of Alexander son of Alexander, the fourteenth year of the satrapship of Ptolemy, in the month Dius. Marriage contract of Heracleides and Demetria. Heracleides takes as his lawful wife Demetria, Coan,[6] both being free-born, from her father Leptines, Coan, and her mother Philotis, bringing clothing and ornaments to the value of one thousand drachma and Heracleides shall supply to Demetria all that is proper for a freeborn wife, and we shall live together wherever it seems best to Leptines and Heracleides consulting in common. If Demetria is discovered doing any evil to the shame of

6 *Coan* means "from the island of Cos."

> her husband Heracleides, she shall be deprived of all that she brought, but Heracleides shall prove whatever he alleges against Demetria before three men whom they both accept. It shall not be lawful for Heracleides to bring home another wife in insult of Demetria nor to have children by another woman nor to do any evil against Demetria on any pretext. If Heracleides is discovered doing any of these things and Demetria proves it before three men whom they both accept, Heracleides shall give back to Demetria the dowry of one thousand drachma which she brought and shall moreover forfeit one thousand drachma of the silver coinage of Alexander. Demetria and those aiding Demetria to exact payment shall have the right of execution, as if derived from a legally decided action, upon the person of Heracleides and upon all the property of Heracleides both on land and on water. This contract shall be valid in every respect, wherever Heracleides may produce it against Demetria, or Demetria and those aiding Demetria to exact payment may produce it against Heracleides, as if the agreement had been made in that place. Heracleides and Demetria shall have the right to keep the contracts severally in their own custody and to produce them against each other. Witnesses: Cleon, Gelan; Anticrates, Temnian; Lysis, Temnian; Dionysius, Temnian; Aristomachus, Cyrenaean; Aristodicus, Coan. (P. Eleph 1 L.1–18)

This very interesting document was not written for a poor couple. In those days, a drachma was apparently a workman's salary for one day. This means that the dowry was a salary for three years of labor. If the man breached the contract, he had to give the dowry back to the bride's family and even double it. The contract even provided an arbitration procedure for complaints. The document was certainly written with care, and it is illuminating to observe what was said and what wasn't: Demetria was the only lawful wife. There could be no other wife, and only her children could inherit their property. But the contract says nothing about what Heracleides could do in brothels or even with his own slaves. Evidently, this was not of interest to the bride's family.

For the most part, we can only speculate how much a dowry actually protected wives. The Roman playwright Plautus, who adapted Greek comedies to Roman audiences, shows that the theme was well-known in Rome too: A husband had to fear that his outraged wife would leave him and take the dowry with her. Housewives could not stop their husbands from having numerous sexual relations, but they could stop them from occurring in their homes. Alcibiades, for instance, seems to have run into problems when he had humiliated his wife by bringing other women into their home: His wife went to the archon (the highest-ranking public official) to demand divorce and, apparently, the dowry (Andocides, *Against Alcibiades*, 14). However, whether or not the dowry actually afforded protection, the wife could be sure of one thing: No other woman could threaten the central power of the lawful wife—that is, to produce legal children.

How Marriage Was Made in Rome

Roman law formed the basis of the Western judiciary system, and even today, law students study some elements of it. Indeed, some of our legal concepts regarding family life are still essentially tied to Roman ideas. For instance, the idea that the father of a child born to a married woman is legally presumed to be the woman's husband is a Roman principle (*pater est quem nuptiae demonstrant*). When it comes to Roman legal conceptions of marriage, it is not always easy to distinguish fact from fiction. The great law collections date from late antiquity, and although they refer to earlier regulations, a historian may have doubts about the age of the laws. The ideals of marriage certainly changed and developed over the centuries, as did the entire society, and the law collections were not designed for historians but for use at that time. It is, then, not an easy task to decipher the laws in force at any given moment in time.

However, the big picture is clear, and it is consistent with Greek practice. Only patricians were full citizens in the oldest era, and only a lawful marriage could produce Roman citizens. That is why it was allowed only for the elite. These patricians entered into marriage by a religious rite (*confarreatio*). Later—but centuries before the Christian era—common people were permitted to get married. *Confarreatio* was still used by nobility, but common people chose between two alternatives: *coemptio* and *usus*. *Coemptio*, "buying," was a formal act in which the bride and her property were immediately transferred to the bridegroom. The alternative was simply to live one year continuously together (*usus*). Both parties could intentionally avoid marriage by *usus* by living outside the house some days every year. This was a way to live together without becoming married.

The word *buying* undoubtedly has negative connotations when referring to marriage, but the Roman housewife actually had a much stronger position than her sisters in Athens. For instance, she could easily divorce her husband. What's more, mutual consent of the couple was a prerequisite for marriage. When this was assured, the bridegroom gave his bride-to-be a ring or a jewel as a sign of betrothal—a custom rather familiar to us.

Since marriage was of central importance to citizenship, it was never unclear whether a couple was married. For the Romans, marriage was a contract with rights and duties. Since it was clear whether one owned the house he lived in, there was no question whether the man was married. A valid contract existed or did not exist.

How Marriage Was Made in Old Testament Times

In the Jewish world, marriage was a very strong institution with deep roots in religion. The first chapter of Scripture tells us how God created the world, established marriage, and blessed the first man and woman:

> And God blessed them. And God said to them, "Be fruitful and multiply and fill the earth and subdue it, and have dominion over the fish of the sea and over the birds of the heavens and over every living thing that moves on the earth." (Genesis 1:28)

The reception history of this verse (that is, its history of interpretation and its influence) is immense. A single man and a single woman, as it has been understood, entered into a union blessed by God. Several texts show that marriage was terminated with a document (Deuteronomy 24:1; Jeremiah 3:8: Isaiah 50:1), which implies that in biblical times, as certainly later, a document was also written when people entered into it.

In times harder than ours, romantic love took a rather distant back seat to staying alive and finding food. In this view, the command that the man who rapes a girl must marry her

(Deuteronomy 22:28–29)—which we would consider a cruel punishment for the poor girl—seems, in fact, designed to protect the girl, her right, and his duty, as strange as it seems to us. Mosaic Law contains another ruling that might look rather strange to modern eyes. If the husband died childless, the brother-in-law had a duty to procreate with the man's widow. The child born was considered a child and heir of the late husband. It was definitely the right of the widow and the duty of the brother-in-law. She had the right to get a child to take care of her and to avoid utmost poverty. Tender feelings mattered less than daily food. If the man refused to fulfill his duty, the widow had the right to publicly spit in his face (Deuteronomy 25:5–10). This kind of procreation, called levirate marriage (*levir* = brother-in-law), was apparently still practiced in Josephus's times, because he rendered the Mosaic rulings quite faithfully (*Antiquities*, 4.254–56); interestingly, Philo, writing in Alexandria, never mentions this law. Judah's son Onan did not want to give offspring to his late brother, but he was cruel enough to misuse the poor widow for his own pleasure, and he got his punishment (Genesis 38:1–10).

The Torah banned marriages between relatives who were too closely related (Leviticus 18). Consequently, John the Baptist criticized Herod's marriage with his sister-in-law and was imprisoned for it (Mark 6:18). When Gentiles already living in such marriages converted to Judaism, Jews probably did not require that the marriage be dissolved, but Paul, for instance, forbade a Christian man to live with his stepmother (1 Corinthians 5).

Sometimes, it is wise not to draw too many conclusions from biblical accounts. For example, when we read the ugly story of how Lot's two daughters gave their father wine and became pregnant by him, we do not really learn anything about the customs of the time. Instead, this story was told to explain the origin of two despicable Gentile peoples, the Moabites and Ammonites (Genesis 19).

Polygamy or Monogamy?

When one reads the Old Testament, one cannot help but notice that the Jewish patriarchs and kings had several wives. Polygamy was self-evident in Eastern cultures. For nomads, having several wives and numerous children made it possible to have large herds. Kings displayed their might by having hundreds of wives, and marriages also served diplomatic relations. In fact, polygamy is clearly present in the Scriptures, and not only in the historical books. The Mosaic Law guaranteed the position of the first wife if the man took another alongside her (Exodus 21:10), and also the rights of the children born to the less-loved wife (Deuteronomy 21:15–17).

Nonetheless, polygamy is not described as the norm established in the creation: The harsh Lamech is the only man who took two wives in the first chapters of Scripture (Genesis 4:19), and his behavior was apparently a consequence of the fall, like the murder of Abel in the same chapter. Scripture also explicitly criticizes polygamy. Song of Solomon 8:12 admires the woman and says,

> My vineyard, my very own, is before me;
> you, O Solomon, may have the thousand,
> and the keepers of the fruit two hundred.

The big picture, then, seems rather clear: God joins a single man with a single woman in the creation and blesses them (Genesis 1:27–28). Later, mostly kings, like David and Solomon, had several wives, as did Herod during Jesus' time.

Samuel's father is the only commoner mentioned as having two wives (1 Samuel 1).

Although Scripture does not ban polygamy, marriage between one man and one woman seemed to take stronger hold across the centuries of the Old Testament. Laban had already warned Jacob not to take more wives besides Laban's two daughters (Genesis 31:50). The praise of a good wife (Proverbs 31:10–31) seems to imply monogamy. God and His people appear in the prophets like a man and a woman in a monogamous marriage (Jeremiah 3; Hosea 2; Ezekiel 16; 24). Nonetheless, polygamy also appears in later sources, and the example of the revered patriarchs made it very difficult for later teachers to explicitly condemn polygamy. Most scholars, however, believe that it was rare in Jesus' time. All in all, it might be useful to open a treasure box a Palestinian cave has delivered to us.

The revolt of Bar-Kochba (AD 132–135) was almost over as the Romans approached the small towns on the shore of the Dead Sea. The leaders of the cities packed their movable property in bags and ran with their families to hide in caves. The Romans found many hidden places and let people starve in the caves. One of the victims was a woman named Babatha, who, like others, had packed her jewels and most important documents, thirty-five in number, in a bag, which scholars found in 1961. One of the twenty skeletons scholars found probably belonged to Babatha. The carefully packed bag, called the Babatha Archive, is, like the rest of the bags, a treasure to scholars. She, a wealthy woman who owned date plantations, was born in about AD 105 and was married for the first time in AD 120 to her cousin Yeshua ben Yeshua at age 15. But she was widowed already in AD 124 and was left with a son named Jesus. In AD 125, she married a man named

Judah, and the bag includes the *ketuba*, the marriage contract of Babatha (see below). Judah died. He had been the husband of two women, Babatha and Miriam, either simultaneously or rather successively. When Babatha fled to the cave, she apparently was married without a written contract to a third man named Eliezer ben Samuel.

The Babatha Archive thus tells us that polygamy may have appeared in Palestine about a century after Jesus, although the case is far from clear. But neither the historian Josephus (*Antiquities*, 4.249–50) nor the rabbis excluded polygamy, at least in principle. What the Patriarchs/Fathers did could not be wrong! But polygamy was often excluded in Jewish marriage contracts in Egypt from the fifth century BC on, and this started to become common in Palestine too. The Septuagint, the Greek translation of the Scriptures made in Egypt, adds the words "these two" in Genesis 2:24, and thus makes monogamy self-evident for the Jews using this translation. This development was not reserved to Greek-speaking Jews, which is shown by the fact that the Qumran community, which did not use the Septuagint, also rejected polygamy (*Temple Scroll*, 57:17–18; *Damascus Covenant*, 4:20–5:2).

All in all, marriage in Israel had gone through many changes before New Testament times. Nonetheless, from the very beginning, marriage belonged to the center of the social fabric in the Hebrew society. "Be fruitful and multiply and fill the earth" (Genesis 1:28) was commonly taken as a command, not a mere blessing, and it meant that everyone had to marry and procreate. This also meant, among other things, that producing children was the primary goal of marriage. Indeed, for some, without children, there was no marriage. For instance, according to Philo, a childless marriage had to be annulled, and he also specified how long the couple could wait for children.

Marriage was thus highly appreciated in early Judaism, and conceiving children was God's command to everyone. It was considered blessed by God, and it belonged not just to the upper class but to everyone. Jews used to marry considerably earlier than Greeks and Romans. Rabbinic texts recommend that girls should marry at puberty and, for example, Mishna, *Abot* 5:21, considers 18 a good age for men to get married. We only have sporadic knowledge of how these ideals were followed in the first Christian century, but the few cases seem to confirm the early age of both sexes.

Early on, Jewish marriage apparently took place in three stages. First, the families agreed on the marriage. Second, the marriage was completed. Finally, it was celebrated.

1. THE DOWRY

Genesis 26 tells us how the family of Rebekah agreed on her marriage. The family asked for her opinion, and this was apparently common. The families also agreed on the price of the bride (*mohar*), often mentioned in the Scripture. It may have been money or goods, but even various services could be used as payment. Jacob worked for fourteen years to get Rachel and Leah (Genesis 29). David had a tougher task. He had to deliver a hundred Philistine foreskins to Saul to marry Saul's daughter Michal (1 Samuel 18).

Greek and Roman customs required the bride's father to use the dowry, paid out of his own money, as protection for his daughter. Jewish fathers, meanwhile, apparently began granting the *mohar*, paid out of the bridegroom's money, to their daughters with a contract that ruled that it was to be paid back in the case of divorce or the death of the husband.

The *mohar*, which was not a small sum, was, then, meant to protect the woman from a harsh destiny. It appeared, however, that young men often lacked the means to pay such sums, and, consequently, marriages were all too often delayed. Neither the bride nor her family was fond of the idea that the young man had to work for several years to save money for the *mohar*. An invention started to save weddings around Jesus' time: The *mohar* was defined, but the total sum could be paid after the wedding. It was mentioned in the marriage contract and paid at divorce or the death of the husband. This way, the intention to protect the girl was preserved, but at the same time, the scheduled payment made the wedding possible. The book of Tobit (7:13) tells how the parties wrote and agreed on a contract. This kind of marriage contract was called a *ketubah*, and we have many examples of them. The Babatha Archive and other bags found in the Cave of Letters include several of them; for example, the document for Babatha's second marriage. The papyrus was written in Aramaic, and it was partly damaged. Judah says in the contract, among others, that he takes Babatha to be his wife "according to the Law of Moses and of the Judeans" (i.e., not according to the Roman law that granted the right to divorce to the wife), admits that he has received four hundred denars as dowry, promises to feed and clothe Babatha, and, if she would be taken captive, redeem her and restore her as his wife (i.e., overlook that she probably would have been raped).

We also see an example of a breached but not annulled marriage contract in a Jewish papyrus from Heracleopolis (*P.Polit. Jud.*, 4). A man named Philotas had engaged a woman named Nicaia in 134 BC, and her father had promised a dowry to her (no mention of *mohar* here). Afterward, however, Nicaia's father had given his daughter to another man, although Philotas had not given her a document annulling their marriage contract. Apparently, the family of the bride did not have the right to cancel the marriage, but the bridegroom did. Philotas thus required—and here we meet the usual problem of the papyrologist: The papyrus is broken, and we must guess what his claim was. Perhaps he demanded the promised dowry. Maybe he demanded the annulment of the new marriage and the entire fulfillment of the contract.

2. THE CONSUMMATION

As we have seen, marriages agreed upon between families may have been long delayed before they were realized. In essence, the realization of a marriage was its consummation. We have some details. Josephus happens to mention sacrifices at the time of the wedding (*Antiquities*, 4.245). The New Testament tells us how the bride and her friends waited with lamps for the bridegroom and his friends (Matthew 25:1–12). He finally arrived and took the bride home. The young couple was brought to the wedding room, and the witnesses waited outside the room. A bloody garment witnessed that the girl had been a virgin, and the parents secured it, as indirectly witnessed in Deuteronomy 22:17–21:

> "And behold, he has accused her of misconduct, saying, 'I did not find in your daughter evidence of virginity.' And yet this is the evidence of my daughter's virginity." And they shall spread the cloak before the elders of the city. Then the elders of that city shall take the man and whip him, and they shall fine him a hundred shekels of silver and give them to the father of the young woman, because he has brought a bad name upon a virgin of Israel. And she shall be

> his wife. He may not divorce her all his days. But if the thing is true, that evidence of virginity was not found in the young woman, then they shall bring out the young woman to the door of her father's house, and the men of her city shall stone her to death with stones, because she has done an outrageous thing in Israel by whoring in her father's house. So you shall purge the evil from your midst.

Modern scholars might ask how old the decrees of the Torah really were and how meticulously people actually followed them. In Jesus' times, observant Jews read these texts in a quite different way from modern scholars. For them, everyone was bound by the commands. The garment was undoubtedly used to show the virginity of the daughter, not necessarily because of any suspicions, but because the Torah said so. Thus, marriages were apparently usually completed among the Jews as described in the Torah. Josephus seems to refer to the practice when writing that a bride who failed to show her virginity was stoned and burned alive if she was the daughter of a priest (*Antiquities*, 4.248).

3. JEWISH MARRIAGE CELEBRATIONS

Scripture often mentions wedding celebrations in passing (as in Psalm 78:16 and Jeremiah 2:32) or as a metaphor of great joy:

> For as a young man marries a young woman,
> so shall your sons marry you,
> and as the bridegroom rejoices over the bride,
> so shall your God rejoice over you. (Isaiah 62:5)

Song of Solomon 4–5 also reflects on the great feast. Nevertheless, the Gospels are our best source on the third phase of the wedding, the celebration. The ten virgins already make it obvious that the wedding feast was not celebrated with only immediate families present. Even more clearly, the wedding at Cana (John 2:1–11) shows how the entire community was invited to celebrate the marriage, and even Jesus and His disciples joined the feast.

Jesus' and the Apostles' Teachings About Marriage

As we've seen, the Old Testament tradition was clear that marriage was established by God. In His teachings, Jesus strongly joined in this tradition:

> But from the beginning of creation, "God made them male and female." "Therefore a man shall leave his father and mother and hold fast to his wife, and the two shall become one flesh." So they are no longer two but one flesh. What therefore God has joined together, let not man separate. (Mark 10:6–9)

Over the centuries, Jesus' parables have brought scenes of the Jewish marriage celebration to Bible readers: The lamps are burning, the bridegroom is coming, and people are ready to start the great feast. Christianity mainly followed Jewish teachings on marriage in the first century. However, there were two important exceptions. From the words of Jesus and Paul already, Christian teaching appreciated life without marriage and rejected divorce (see chapter 5 and chapter 9).

In Jesus' words about marriage, the debate with the Sadducees is worth noting. The Sadducees told Jesus a story about a woman who had been married to seven men and had been widowed without children each time. So, whose wife would she be after the resurrection? Jesus harshly answered,

> Is this not the reason you are wrong, because you know neither the Scriptures nor the power of God? For when they rise from the dead, they neither marry nor are given in marriage, but are like angels in heaven. (Mark 12:24–25).

The imaginary story of the Sadducees was, of course, meant to mock the very idea of resurrection. Nonetheless, Jesus' answer shows something important about the nature of marriage. For Jewish writers who waited for the Messiah, life in a messianic era was presumed to resemble their current life, even though it was, of course, to be much happier. Jesus, however, shows that marriage belongs exclusively to our world, or at least that eternal life cannot be described as an improved version of the earthly village life. The coming era is entirely different, and we should not think of it as something framed by our own experience of family life.

In the New Testament, marriage was entered into according to Jewish practices. First, there was an agreement; second, there was consummation; and, finally, there was a celebration.

Accordingly, when Mary and Joseph were "engaged," the marriage was promised, and a contract was apparently written, but the marriage was not completed. Joseph had agreed to pay a sum of money to Mary's family, or more probably, promised to pay it at a possible divorce, since he probably didn't have the means to pay the money up front. However, because Mary was pregnant, the planned marriage was going to be canceled, and the terms of cancellation were being studied. Essentially, Joseph had two options: (1) state that Mary had had premarital sex with another man and breached the contract in this way—whatever the consequences for her, he was not going to uphold his side of the contract and pay the price for the bride—or (2) take the blame for the cancellation and pay what the contract required, even though he wasn't going to marry Mary. According to the Gospels, Joseph was going to choose the second option. Since this amounted to both taking blame for what he hadn't done and paying for what he wasn't going to get, this shows a very commendable character. Presumably, he was going to do it because it was much kinder for Mary. However, a heavenly visit changed his mind, and the rest is history.

The consummation and celebration of marriage often appear in Jesus' speeches and parables. The ten virgins and "the friend of the bridegroom" in John 3:29 were apparently waiting outside the house and subsequently witnessed when the garment was put aside to be preserved by the family of the bride as proof. The wedding at Cana, with the vast amount of wine, shows how the entire community, with friends living elsewhere and even Jesus with a dozen of His followers, were invited to the feast.

So, in sum, marriage was a very strong institution in the New Testament world. We know only a little of how the first Christians entered into their marriages: Ignatius says that the couples married with the consent of the bishop (*Letter to Polycarp*, 5). A passage in Tertullian lets us understand that the contract was written in the presence of the pastor, and the couple was blessed by him (see above). As both Jews and Greeks or Romans, they certainly knew whether they were married. For most Greeks and Romans, a carefully formulated document made it clear, and this was apparently usual among

Jews as well. It is highly probable that the first Christians followed this path. Whatever the exact manner, the letter to the Hebrews uses strong words:

> Let marriage (γάμος, *gamos*) be held in honor among all, and let the marriage bed be undefiled, for God will judge the sexually immoral and adulterous. (Hebrews 13:4)

The word γάμος, *gamos*, can denote "marriage," but the first impression is "wedding feast." Furthermore, for Christians, the wedding feast took on additional importance as a beautiful, mysterious metaphor. The last chapters of the book of Revelation describe the beginning of the upcoming, long-expected party: the celestial wedding feast.

Reflection Questions

- Marriage has long been a significant institution across cultures. Explain why you think that is.

- Christians often question when marriage truly begins. What insight does this chapter provide?

- Imagine yourself as a woman or man in a Greek or Roman marriage. How would you feel compared to being a husband or a wife today?

7

Only to Have Children? Sex Within Jewish and Christian Marriage

The reason for marriage in the Greek and Roman world centered on the need to get lawful heirs, and marriage hardly prevented extramarital sex for men. It consequently does not make much sense to ask if children were the only morally accepted goal of marital sex. Ascetic ideals grew more and more popular and certainly also influenced sexual ideals. Nevertheless, I am not aware of any discussions on the topic in the Greco-Roman world. It was, however, relevant both in Jewish and Christian contexts. Now we also must ask if contraception was allowed among them.

Ancient Contraception

Contraception has, during the last sixty years, changed our culture more than we understand. The use of contraception was not as simple in classical antiquity as it is today, but it was also not as ineffective as scholars have believed until recent decades. Until recently, scholars may have made their audience laugh by quoting Pliny, the man who indeed had an interest in nature and plants:

> It is certain that pregnant women must avoid a raven's egg, since if they step over it they will miscarry through the mouth. (*Natural History*, 30:130)

Modern people who laugh at ancient medicine might, however, not know that it included two paths: one relying on magic, and another based on a surprisingly accurate knowledge of human anatomy. Although ancient medicine was on a high level, as Hippocrates, Soranus, and Galenus show, it had misjudged the most fertile days for women, which made birth control by the rhythm method impossible. Consequently, modern scholars long considered ancient contraception totally ineffective. John Riddle, however, turned the tide with his work *Contraception and Abortion from the Ancient World to the Renaissance* (Harvard University Press, 1994). He tested ancient recipes on guinea pigs and mice. The medicines caused total infertility and even early abortion in up to 80 percent of cases. Results of human tests are not available as far as I know. Nevertheless, the drugs were hardly totally ineffective.

As we discussed above, governments rarely got mixed up in family life but allowed individuals to freely make their own decisions. Contraception did not usually bother governments, and conventional morals did not ban it. It might rather have been even preferred because it reduced the exposure of children, which was considered a sad necessity.

Jewish Teachings on Contraception

It is interesting to ask what Jews taught about contraception. Marriage was usually considered a duty, and procreation was taken as a command, not only a blessing. It was a command to be honored. For childless men, Genesis 1:28 constituted a sexual duty, which was, perhaps not without humor, expounded on with great detail in the Mishna:

> He who takes a vow not to have sexual relations with his wife—the House of Shammai says " [he may allow this situation to continue] for two weeks." And the House of Hillel say, "For one week." Disciples go forth for Torah study without [the wife's] consent for thirty days. Workers go out for one week. "The sexual duty of which the Torah speaks: Those without work [of independent means]—every day: workers—twice a week; ass drivers—once a week; camel drivers—once in thirty days; sailors—once in six months," the words of R. Eliezer. (Mishna, *Ketubot* 5:6)

Nevertheless, the command could be fulfilled. Jewish teachers interpreted it variously, and rabbinic collections quoted several interpretations:

> A man should not give up having sexual relations unless he has children. The House of Shammai says, "Two boys." And the House of Hillel says, "A boy and a girl," since it is said "Male and female he created them." (Mishna, *Yebamot* 6:6)

Teachers gave strict orders on some questions, but this one, like many others, was different, and there was room for various opinions. It is easy to see that it was, according to many teachers, possible to fulfill the command to procreate. The Tosefta also quotes different opinions on the number of children, sometimes also including the grandchildren. The death of a child reinstated the duty (Tosefta, *Yebamot* 8:4).

So, the command could be fulfilled, but what did it mean when it was fulfilled? Was the couple expected to end their sex life, or was contraception allowed now? The Mishna at least once (Mishna, *Yebamot* 6:6) says that the command to procreate was only given to men ("the man is required to be fruitful and multiply but not the woman"). Did it mean that contraception was free for women? R. Judah is said to have spoken more leniently about birth control for women (Tosefta, *Yebamot* 8:4). The redactors of the Mishna and the Tosefta could include this kind of opinion in the collections of authoritative Jewish interpretations.

Procreation or Pleasure?

Jews greatly appreciated marriage. God had created mankind male and female, and marriage was His gift. Many Jewish teachers, however, were critical of sex without the intention to procreate. Philo banned marital sex if procreation was impossible or difficult, as in an infertile marriage or if a man married an older woman. He explained the ban during menstruation by the fact that the woman could not conceive during those days (*On the Special Laws*, 3:32). Only pigs and goats have sex for pleasure (*On the Special Laws*, 3:112–14).

Josephus does not hesitate here to play with double cards. He makes Joseph give a long speech to Mrs. Potiphar and tells her to enjoy sex with her own husband (who was a eunuch!; *Antiquities*, 2.50–52). But he also praises the Essenes, whose married couples did not have sex if the wife was pregnant because they believed that the goal of sex was not pleasure but procreation (*War*, 2:161). When proudly presenting the Jewish marriage laws, he claims that this was the manner of life of all Jews (*Apion*, 2.199–203). According to the Mishna, sex should only be repeated after three days (i.e., every second day, as we would count it; Mishna, *Shabbat* 9:3; Mishna, *Miqvaot* 8:3). According to the *Testament of Issachar*, Leah got only six children instead of eight because she sought pleasure in sex and was punished.

These passages were written for Jewish readers, but some of them also sought a Greek and Roman audience. Jewish teachers liked to present the Jewish disciplined manner of life and assumed that their Gentile readers would appreciate it. This shows how ascetic ideals lived in the Greco-Roman world and how they grew stronger in imperial times. Marriage was certainly appreciated, but passions of the body were not to rule over the soul, and sexual pleasure was not an exception.

Early Christians and Contraception

But what did early Christians say about contraception? We have no word of it in the New Testament, and the silence goes on until the third century. The first text briefly addressing the topic is *Octavius* by Minucius Felix (early third century AD).

> And I see that you at one time expose your begotten children to wild beasts and to birds; at another, that you crush them when strangled with a miserable kind of death. There are some women who, by drinking medical preparations, extinguish the source of the future man in their very bowels, and thus commit a parricide before they bring forth. (*Octavius*, 30)

Medicaments caused both contraception and abortion, and the target of criticism is unclear. Was the writer banning abortion or contraception or both? The fog soon disappeared, and Christian teachers unequivocally banned contraception. Hippolytus, Jerome, and Augustine, for example, condemned voluntary infertility. They taught that this should be linked with the strong appreciation of virginity and single life. If teachers struggled to wholeheartedly accept that marriage and children were the only legitimate goals for sex, contraception had no role. Only a few church fathers recognized other goals for marital sex. This big picture made it clear that contraception was not allowed—not in marital and especially not in extramarital sex.

Virginity was gold, marriage was silver, and sex for pleasure alone was too much. I only know of some exceptions. Lactantius (*Divine Institutes*, 6:20) allowed a man to have sex with his pregnant wife and even attributed it to the good Creator that the wife wanted to go on having sex with her husband. Nevertheless, he also considered children the only goal for marital sex (*Institutes*, 6:23), as Justin Martyr had said earlier (*1 Apol.*, 29). Clement of Alexandria, who strongly defended marriage, joined the choir (*Stromateis*, 2.18:92–93), claiming that the Mosaic Law banned a man from having sex with his wife while she was pregnant or breastfeeding. Clement, who had accurately studied the works by Philo, also repeated his comments on pigs and goats (*Stromateis*, 2.23:144; *SC*, 38: 142; 3.11:71–72; *GCS*, 15:228). A Christian husband should not, according to Athanagoras, sow more than is needed for procreation (*Plea for Christians*, 33).

Is Sexual Passion Within Marriage a Sin?

Augustine strongly rejected the view that marriage is a sin. For him, procreation was not the only legitimate goal of marital sex, because it also prevented adultery. Nevertheless, sexual passion was, according to him, sinful also within marriage. Passion is always a sin, but within marriage, it is a venial sin. Every Christian man hopes, according to Augustine, that procreation can happen without passion, as men put corn in the field (*City of God*, 14:23). Contraception makes marriage a brothel and the father-in-law a pimp (*Nupt. et conc.*, 1.15:17; *CSEL*, 42:230). Augustine was apparently well aware of the topic. He had lived with a woman for thirteen years, and this concubinage produced only one single son, Adeodatus. When his mother, a committed Christian, ended the concubinage to seek a noble wife for her son, he still took another concubine (*Confessions*, 6:15). The goal for this kind of relationship was not to get children, and especially not to get lawful heirs. Concubines had to go when men started to seek marriages compatible with their social status.

This all means that both early Judaism and subsequently early Christianity overlooked important Old Testament passages. The literal interpretation of Song of Solomon was an abomination for Augustine (*De Spiritu et Littera*, 4). Nevertheless, it was originally a beautiful love song praising the sexual pleasures of marriage. The early interpretation of these poems speaks of love between God and His people, and the book would not have been accepted into the canon without this interpretation. Proverbs strongly warns young men of extramarital relations and shows a better way:

> Drink water from your own cistern,
> flowing water from your own well.

> Should your springs be scattered abroad,
> streams of water in the streets?
> Let them be for yourself alone,
> and not for strangers with you.
> Let your fountain be blessed,
> and rejoice in the wife of your youth,
> a lovely deer, a graceful doe.
> Let her breasts fill you at all times with delight;
> be intoxicated always in her love.
> Why should you be intoxicated, my son, with a forbidden woman and embrace the bosom of an adulteress? (Proverbs 5:15–20)

Paul also gives a piece of advice that caused many explanations by later church fathers:

> Now concerning the matters about which you wrote: "It is good for a man not to have sexual relations with a woman." But because of the temptation to sexual immorality, each man should have his own wife and each woman her own husband. The husband should give to his wife her conjugal rights, and likewise the wife to her husband. For the wife does not have authority over her own body, but the husband does. Likewise the husband does not have authority over his own body, but the wife does. Do not deprive one another, except perhaps by agreement for a limited time, that you may devote yourselves to prayer; but then come together again, so that Satan may not tempt you because of your lack of self-control.
>
> Now as a concession, not a command, I say this. I wish that all were as I myself am. But each has his own

gift from God, one of one kind and one of another. (1 Corinthians 7:1–7)

Paul greatly appreciates single life but shows that marriage has several functions. Termination of marital sex increases the danger of extramarital relations. But Paul also writes that both members of the couple have duties to their spouse. He rather surprisingly says that the husband does not have authority over his own body but yields it to his wife. Marital sex is obviously not a necessary evil here, and procreation is not the only goal for it.

Societies only slowly update family values that are centuries old or more. Biology has, until recent days, dictated that sex may make a woman pregnant contrary to her will. This produced values that said a decent woman should not have sex before marriage. Contraception and abortion, lawful in many countries, have changed the facts since the 1960s. Those methods allowed women to fearlessly live as men had always lived. This dramatic change challenged Christian churches everywhere. Premarital sex, as well as living together before marriage, has become usual, even a norm. Nevertheless, the old values have not completely disappeared. Numerous sex partners have traditionally hurt the reputation of women more than that of men, but we are apparently approaching the point at which numerous sex contacts label neither men nor women. What is our reaction? Is everything okay now, or do we have more to say?

Reflection Questions

- Both the early Jews and Christians had a strong belief that children were the only honest goal for sex; any other goal was sinful. Is there a Bible-based reason to think God intended more? Or have we only assimilated to our environment when we think desire and pleasure in married sex is good?

- Reflect on the manner in which contraception has changed our world. Do you consider it good, bad, or both?

- Some married couples are never able to have children. How can we help them?

- Some married couples are childless by their own decision. What do you think about such an idea?

8

ADULTERY: ABOUT MORALS AND LACK OF MORALS

Traditional churches have suffered heavy losses in modern Western societies. This has especially led older people to speak of a "lack of morals" as the cause. This is mostly a mistake. The problem is not a lack of morals, but that society's morals have rapidly changed. An immoral person acts against her or his own values. Such people exist and have always existed, but a moral code and social control have not disappeared from our world. The main question is, what was considered right and wrong in ancient times and what is considered right and wrong today? So what about adultery? The term *adultery* here does not include premarital or all extramarital sex but sex with a married person. It is precisely here where it is interesting to ask how Greeks and Romans used to live.

ANCIENT GREEK AND ROMAN VIEWS ON ADULTERY

Horace describes what might have happened if a man were caught in adultery in Rome. The outraged husband stands at the door, the dogs are barking, and the slave girl, aware of the affair, starts to cry, knowing that the master will crush her legs. If the man fails to flee, the male servants will catch him, and it is better for the sake of shame to leave untold what happens next (*Epistles*, 1:2).

More serious texts show that the fate of the man caught in adultery was no better in Athens. The very early laws by Draco allowed the husband to kill the man caught in the act (*Demosthenes*, 23:53; Lysias, 1:30–31). Aristophanes, using much softer words than Horace (*Clouds*, 1067–85), writes that people stuffed vegetables into the man's anus.

Sexual needs should thus not be fulfilled in the bed of neighbors. Horace referred to approving words by Cato, the strict moralist, upon meeting a young man coming from a brothel. Horace himself said that a slave girl or boy was enough for him when his craving sought a target. It is important to understand that the entire satire is deeply moral and restrictive: The poet told Roman youth to leave married women alone. There were also other kinds of poets, and not far from Horace. Augustus expelled his colleague Ovid from Rome because of a scandal not known to us in detail; he never allowed him to return to the city. He had crossed the limits of conventional morals, and his *Tristia* did not soften the heart of Caesar.

Previous chapters have shown that a Greek or Roman husband was not expected to be faithful to his wife as we understand the term. The standards for the wife were, however, totally different. She could not limit the life of her husband, but the husband did not want to share his wife with other men. Adultery was not accepted, neither for a wife nor a husband. It did not mean that everyone followed the moral code, as the poems of Ovidius and Martialis, for example, clearly show. Many poets might have been adulterers, but there were plenty of other people too. Noble Romans divorced their wives because they had been unfaithful, as Pompeius did. And when Gaius Julius Caesar, the hero, arrived in Rome, his soldiers used the freedom for the triumph allowed to them: "Men of Rome, keep close to your consorts, here's a bald adulterer" (Suetonius, *Julius Caesar*, 51). The propaganda used by Caesar's opponents certainly targeted him with malicious rumors, but it was clear that he was a real playboy and adulterer. Nevertheless, conventional morals said to avoid married women.

Scriptural Teachings on Adultery

Jewish and Christian instruction indeed overlapped Gentile morals. The Sixth Commandment strongly bans adultery:

> You shall not commit adultery. (Exodus 20:14)

The Sixth Commandment is clear, and neither men nor women needed explanations for it. Jews used to marry early, and that is why adultery was the most common sexual offense. Scripture often uses marriage to describe the connection between God and Israel—the people serving idols and overlooking His commandments act like an adulterous wife (Jeremiah 3; Hosea 1–3). When Jesus allegorically speaks of an "evil and adulterous generation" (Matthew 16:4), we first understand that marriage must be holy and that this is applied to how we must deal with God.

The book of Proverbs contains fewer bans and commandments and mainly lets wisdom call people to the right path. We note two passages:

> So you will be delivered from the forbidden woman,
> from the adulteress with her smooth words,

who forsakes the companion of her youth
    and forgets the covenant of her God;
for her house sinks down to death,
    and her paths to the departed. (Proverbs 2:16–18)

My son, keep your father's commandment,
    and forsake not your mother's teaching.
Bind them on your heart always;
    tie them around your neck.
When you walk, they will lead you;
    when you lie down, they will watch over you;
    and when you awake, they will talk with you.
For the commandment is a lamp and the teaching
a light,
    and the reproofs of discipline are the way of life,
to preserve you from the evil woman,
    from the smooth tongue of the adulteress.
Do not desire her beauty in your heart,
    and do not let her capture you with her eyelashes;
for the price of a prostitute is only a loaf of bread,
    but a married woman hunts down a precious life.
Can a man carry fire next to his chest
    and his clothes not be burned?
Or can one walk on hot coals
    and his feet not be scorched?
So is he who goes in to his neighbor's wife;
    none who touches her will go unpunished.
People do not despise a thief if he steals
    to satisfy his appetite when he is hungry,
but if he is caught, he will pay sevenfold;
    he will give all the goods of his house.
He who commits adultery lacks sense;

he who does it destroys himself.
He will get wounds and dishonor,
and his disgrace will not be wiped away.
For jealousy makes a man furious,
and he will not spare when he takes revenge.
He will accept no compensation;
he will refuse though you multiply gifts.
(Proverbs 6:20–35)

Early Jewish Teachings

Early Jewish writings told people to strictly honor the Mosaic ruling on adultery. Works written around Jesus' time show that writers believed that it antedated Moses. The book of Jubilees tells how Joseph, molested by the wife of Potiphar, remembered "what his father Jacob read to him as words of Abraham" (*Book of Jubilees*, 39:6–7), and the *Testament of Joseph* repeats the idea (*Testament of Joseph*, 3). Philo lets Joseph teach Mrs. Potiphar and simultaneously his own readers:

> What would be my inward feelings if I agreed to this unholy act? What my looks when I face him, iron-hearted though I be? No, conscience will take hold of me and not suffer me to look him straight in the face even if I can escape detection. And that cannot be, for there are thousands to sit in judgement on my secret doings who must not remain silent; not to mention that, even if no other knows of it or reports the knowledge which he shares with me, all the same I shall turn informer against myself through my color, my look, my voice, convicted as I said just now by my conscience. And even if no one denounce me, have we

> no fear of respect for justice, the assessor of God, justice who surveys all our doings? (*De Iosepho*, 47–48)

Josephus also summarizes the Mosaic Law and Jewish manner of life to his Gentile readers. He twice says that a man caught in adultery gets the death sentence (*Apion*, 2.201, 215), as do rapists and anyone who touches a betrothed woman.

Christian Views on Adultery

There is no need to use several pages to tell what the first Christians thought about adultery. Jesus often self-evidently condemned it, as in the Sermon on the Mount:

> You have heard that it was said, "You shall not commit adultery." But I say to you that everyone who looks at a woman with lustful intent has already committed adultery with her in his heart. If your right eye causes you to sin, tear it out and throw it away. For it is better that you lose one of your members than that your whole body be thrown into hell. And if your right hand causes you to sin, cut it off and throw it away. For it is better that you lose one of your members than that your whole body go into hell. (Matthew 5:27–30)

Jesus, however, met people who had sinned in different ways. A fragment transmitted in the Gospel of John tells about a woman caught in adultery (John 8:1–11). Preachers sometimes "know" that furious men had allowed the man to flee and only caught the poor woman. If we start this kind of guesswork, the texts presented above would rather make me assume that the man's life had suddenly ended.

The early church followed Jesus and banned adultery, apparently making clear at the moment of Baptism that adulterers would not inherit the kingdom of God (1 Corinthians 6:9–11). The letter to the Hebrews says that God will judge the adulterer and all the sexually immoral (Hebrews 13:4). There was no need for long reasoning, because both Greco-Roman and Jewish morals banned adultery. The early church fathers self-evidently banned adultery, especially when presenting Christians as ideal people (*Letter to Diognetus*, 5; Minucius Felix, *Octavius*, 36).

A wise saying tells Christians to read two books—the Bible and the book the Creator has written on the heart of every human being. The common sense of morals concerning adultery was evident for Gentiles as well as for Christians. Many ideals have faded over the centuries, but sex with the wife or husband of another person is still unacceptable according to most modern people. People are not keen to share their spouse with other people. Today we ask if this ideal will survive the next decades.

Time has not destroyed Christian morals in general, and especially not at this point. Adultery has hurt and still hurts, as those who have shed endless tears over it know best. God, as Christians say, loves us, and that is why He has, with His rulings, protected the most sensitive areas of the hearts of our dearest and of our own. Love needs limits, here if anywhere.

Reflection Questions

- What are the current moral standards in your country? How prevalent are they? How have you seen them change over time?

- Values change, but betrayal and adultery still hurt. Why do you think that is?

- What do younger generations consider right and wrong? How is that different or similar to what older generations consider right and wrong?

9

Wrecked! Ending Marriage

Not all married couples continue on their common path in days of joy and adversity until death parts them. This chapter discusses how marriage was terminated in ancient days.

Abandonment or Divorce?

It is useful to distinguish between *abandonment* and *divorce*. *Abandonment* means that the husband (always the case in the ancient world as far as I know) sent away his wife, who did not have a similar option. That was the case in ancient Israel, where a woman could hardly have had an independent life outside of her family. Although Ruth was not abandoned but widowed, the reader of the beautiful book of Ruth understands her desperate situation. *Divorce* means that both spouses have a similar option. It is most appropriate to speak of *abandonment* in the ancient world. Nevertheless, trade, options to work outside one's own farm (as a weaver or someone in the fishing industry), and small industry transformed Mediterranean societies, and women may have been wealthy and independent, like Lydia and Phoebe in Acts and the letters of Paul. The volcanic eruption that suddenly ended life in Pompeii let modern scholars study the ruins and understand how women's lives greatly differed from earlier times, and now *divorce* is, in many cases, the appropriate word.

Divorce in Ancient Greece and Rome

We know most about the practices during the classical period in Greece from Athenian sources, but even here we must wonder how selective the sources were. We only know about ten cases, and they show that it was easy for a man to end the marriage. The wife, and principally her family, were also allowed to end the marriage. The small number of cases indicates that citizens quite rarely ended their marriage, probably because marriage also connected the privileged families of the city and divorce often left deep wounds in the city. Marriage was a strong institution in Athens, and apparently also in other Greek cities.

The marriage ceremony that produced citizens (*confarreatio*) was reserved for Roman nobility in ancient times, and it was difficult to terminate a marriage without a strong reason. If men sent their wives away, they referred to adultery, the murder of their own children, or similar offenses. Later, however, marriages were often ended, and nobles may still have referred to adultery. But people frequently divorced and remarried in late Republican and Imperial Rome, and women were often the active ones filing for a divorce. No reason was mentioned when Paulla Valeria ended her marriage after her husband returned from the province. She married another nobleman (Cicero, *Ad familiares*, 8, 7). Cicero's own daughter married three times, Pompeius married five times, and a writing on a tombstone tells how a woman had been married to no less than seven men. Martialis (6:7) mocked a lady named Telesilla, who rapidly entered into her tenth marriage. Marriage was for such people rather a contract securing the juridic part of their current relationship. It was terminated quickly and without a feeling of shame, and the woman could be the active one, at least among the nobility.

Divorce in the Old Testament

The Torah includes this ruling:

> When a man takes a wife and marries her, if then she finds no favor in his eyes because he has found some indecency in her, and he writes her a certificate of divorce and puts it in her hand and sends her out of his house . . . (Deuteronomy 24:1–4)

The husband clearly sends his wife away and abandons her, but there is no rule giving such an option to the wife. The husband was told to give his wife a document, which made her a free woman. This "certificate of divorce" sometimes appears in Scripture (Isaiah 50:1; Jeremiah 3:8). Prophets often called Israel and Judah adulterers for serving foreign gods and told how such wives would be sent away (Jeremiah 3; Ezra 10:16–44), certainly reflecting practices in their society.

The book of Malachi mainly consists of debates between the prophet and his opponents, who apparently were priests hypocritically serving in the temple. The book often follows a clear structure: The prophet utters a claim, which is subsequently questioned by his opponents, and the real message follows this denial. In Malachi 2, it goes as follows:

> And this second thing you do. You cover the LORD's altar with tears, with weeping and groaning because

> He no longer regards the offering or accepts it with favor from your hand. But you say, "Why does He not?" Because the LORD was witness between you and the wife of your youth, to whom you have been faithless, though she is your companion and your wife by covenant. Did He not make them one, with a portion of the Spirit in their union? And what was the one God seeking? Godly offspring. So guard yourselves in your spirit, and let none of you be faithless to the wife of your youth. "For the man who does not love his wife but divorces her, says the LORD, the God of Israel, covers his garment with violence, says the LORD of hosts. So guard yourselves in your spirit, and do not be faithless." (vv. 13–16)

The text of verse 15 is probably corrupted beyond repair, and it is translated differently in every translation, old and modern. It is unnecessary here to present all the attempts to solve the problem. However, nothing blurs the main message of the passage. It is a severe sin for the husband to send his wife away. Scripture thus seems sometimes to allow divorce, at least to men, but also sometimes criticizes it. What did early Jewish texts say?

Deuteronomy orders a man to give the woman a document of divorce, and this very brief ruling also implies quite a lot. First, marriage was started and ended with a document. Second, the ruling seems to permit terminating the marriage exclusively to men, and this view is attested in rabbinic texts. Nevertheless, women were also active here well before Jesus' time, as documented in some texts (*P. Se'elim*, 13). But religious authorities could also find a way to allow the wife to divorce her husband without offending their literal interpretation of the Torah. Mishna, *Arakhin* 5:6, says that a court may compel a man to allow his wife to divorce him. The husband may have offended the marriage contract, beat his wife, or refused to procreate, but he could refuse to divorce her, and, as the Torah passage was interpreted, no meant no. But the court could "compel" him—whatever that included—until his no turned to yes. Philo, who wrote in Alexandria, did not like divorces requested by women but considered them possible (*On the Special Laws*, 30). Wealthy Jewish women could apply Roman law instead of the Jewish rulings and so get what they wanted.

Early Jewish Teachings on Divorce

But what did Deuteronomy mean by the words "because he has found some indecency in her"? Early Jewish teachers interpreted the words differently. As scholars traditionally present, the House of Shammai only approved a divorce when the wife had committed adultery ("only because he has found ground for it in unchastity"), while every fault—such as she had spoiled a dish—was enough for the House of Hillel (Mishna, *Gittin* 9:10). The Law thus required that the man had a reason for the divorce, but this could be, according to Hillel's interpretation, practically anything. These are principles, but we also have documents telling about the divorces of individuals. They, like the marriage contracts, show that wealthy women could also refer to secular laws to get the divorce they wanted.

Josephus was married three times, and according to him, men could terminate the marriage for any reason, "and many such arise among human beings" (*Antiquities*, 4.253). Jews, like other people, used to write marriage contracts, and such contracts could also be canceled. Although rabbinic sources tell another story, mainline Judaism seems to have allowed this both to men and women, and Josephus quite clearly says that his wife left him (*Vita*, 416). Nevertheless, Paul writes to the mainly Jewish Roman Church that a married woman is bound by law to her husband as long as he is alive (Romans 7:1–3). He thus knew the tradition that did not allow women to divorce. But did it allow men to divorce?

JESUS' TEACHINGS ON DIVORCE

Marriage and remarriage were a burning issue in early Judaism. When a Galilean teacher moved to Jerusalem to fulfill His mission, one of the first questions He was asked was about marriage.

> And He left there and went to the region of Judea and beyond the Jordan, and crowds gathered to Him again. And again, as was His custom, He taught them.
>
> And Pharisees came up and in order to test Him asked, "Is it lawful for a man to divorce his wife?" He answered them, "What did Moses command you?" They said, "Moses allowed a man to write a certificate of divorce and to send her away." And Jesus said to them, "Because of your hardness of heart he wrote you this commandment. But from the beginning of creation, 'God made them male and female.' 'Therefore a man shall leave his father and mother and hold fast to his wife, and the two shall become one flesh.' So they are no longer two but one flesh. What therefore God has joined together, let not man separate."
>
> And in the house the disciples asked Him again about this matter. And He said to them, "Whoever divorces

> his wife and marries another commits adultery against her, and if she divorces her husband and marries another, she commits adultery." (Mark 10:1–12)

Jesus' words are clear, even painfully clear for the church. He was asked for a statement: Which one of the two Jewish traditions had He adopted? Here, as so often, He took a completely new path and said that Moses' intention was to help women. He did not allow abandonment but protected the woman when the godless husband threw her out. At minimum, he must give her a document making her a free woman and so giving her a distant option to marry again. Jesus' words, as Mark has them, strictly deny that a man has the right to abandon his wife and rather resemble the words of Malachi quoted above. The next words apply this also to the wife, which means that the debate that started from abandonment ended with words on divorce.

Matthew, who in general knew the Jewish debate very well, adds to the question the words "to divorce one's wife *for any cause*?" (Matthew 19:3, emphasis added). He also adds something to Jesus' answer in Mark:

> And I say to you: whoever divorces his wife, except for sexual immorality, and marries another, commits adultery. (Matthew 19:9)

The words have been problematic to interpreters, and they have asked what was permitted here: Only to end the marriage, or also to marry again? We will return to this question in chapter 10.

The Apostles' Teachings

As told above (Romans 7:1–3), Paul, in passing, says that divorce is not allowed (for women?), but the most important passage about this in his letters is in 1 Corinthians 7:10–16:

> To the married I give this charge (not I, but the Lord): the wife should not separate from her husband (but if she does, she should remain unmarried or else be reconciled to her husband), and the husband should not divorce his wife.
>
> To the rest I say (I, not the Lord) that if any brother has a wife who is an unbeliever, and she consents to live with him, he should not divorce her. If any woman has a husband who is an unbeliever, and he consents to live with her, she should not divorce him. For the unbelieving husband is made holy because of his wife, and the unbelieving wife is made holy because of her husband. Otherwise your children would be unclean, but as it is, they are holy. But if the unbelieving partner separates, let it be so. In such cases the brother or sister is not enslaved. God has called you to peace. For how do you know, wife, whether you will save your husband? Or how do you know, husband, whether you will save your wife?

Verses 10–11 are clear, and Paul refers to Jesus' words: A wife must not leave her husband, and a husband must not leave his wife. If they cannot live together, both must remain single. If the Gospel causes problems in a marriage, the Christian party must not depart. If the non-Christian party departs, the Christian is free. We will discuss what this means in chapter 10. Paul does not speak about abandonment but divorce, because the ruling binds both the husband and the wife. Women like Phoebe and Lydia, who played a drastically different role than their sisters in the times of Ruth, were thus told not to leave their men, although the Gentile law allowed them to do it.

Early Christian Teachings

A very early Christian voice, the *Shepherd of Hermas* (early second century AD), not only allowed but required divorce for a man if his wife was caught in adultery and did not repent, because he otherwise became responsible for her sin. As we will see in chapter 10, this did not mean that the man was free to marry again (*Shepherd of Hermas*, 29). Early Christian fathers were otherwise adamant here. If Papinianus (the great Roman lawyer) and Paul disagreed, a Christian must follow Paul, as Jerome formulated the common opinion of the fathers (*Epistle*, 77:3).

The words of Jesus and Paul were clear enough, and they led the Christians during the next centuries to meet the world as their Jewish predecessors had met it earlier. The Gentile legislation differed still more from Christian norms than from the Torah. The instruction was clear for centuries. It is more difficult to describe real life in Christian Europe before the Reformation.

Reflection Questions

- The Old Testament refers to *abandonment* as the stronger spouse sending away the weaker. Is this possible today?

- For Romans and ancient Jews, marriage was a cancelable contract. How does this compare to Christian marriage?

- Numerous divorces are an open wound in our churches. What can we do to support marriages?

10

A New Love?

The texts quoted in the previous chapter show that it was not difficult for a man or a woman to end their marriage and remarry in Greece or Rome. Marriages were made and terminated often, and a seventh or even a tenth marriage was not a problem. But how were divorce and remarriage treated among Jews and Christians?

Old Testament Teachings on Remarriage

The Mosaic ruling quoted above speaks of an abandoned wife, and the next verses tell how life could go on:

> When a man takes a wife and marries her, if then she finds no favor in his eyes because he has found some indecency in her, and he writes her a certificate of divorce and puts it in her hand and sends her out of his house, and she departs out of his house, and if she goes and becomes another man's wife, and the latter man hates her and writes her a certificate of divorce and puts it in her hand and sends her out of his house, or if the latter man dies, who took her to be his wife, then her former husband, who sent her away, may not take her again to be his wife, after she

> has been defiled, for that is an abomination before the LORD. And you shall not bring sin upon the land that the LORD your God is giving you for an inheritance. (Deuteronomy 24:1–4)

A man was not allowed to just throw his wife out, but the man was told to give her a document making her free from him. She could thus remarry, and the only limit was that she could not return to her former husband after remarriage. That is exactly what happens in the book of Hosea, where the prophet's marriage is compared to God and Israel. Otherwise, the Law did not limit remarriage at all.

Early Judaism also allowed a new marriage. Josephus had married three times. Marriage contracts mentioned in the previous chapter and other nonliterary sources show that people got divorced and remarried. Marriage was made with a contract, and it was possible to cancel the contract.

Jesus' Teachings on Remarriage

What Jesus said about abandonment, divorce, and new marriage greatly differed from both Greco-Roman and Jewish ideas. Jesus seems to totally ban remarriage in the Gospel of Mark:

> And in the house the disciples asked Him again about this matter. And He said to them, "Whoever divorces his wife and marries another commits adultery against her, and if she divorces her husband and marries another, she commits adultery." (10:10–12).

These words seem to leave nothing to discuss. We must, however, observe the words Matthew adds to Mark's words:

> And I say to you: whoever divorces his wife, except for sexual immorality (μὴ ἐπὶ πορνείᾳ, *mē epi porneia*), and marries another, commits adultery. (Matthew 19:9)

Do these words mean that a husband (as in the verse) may abandon his adulterous wife *and* marry another woman? Or does Jesus allow abandonment but not a new marriage? And does the word *porneia* only mean adultery as we understand it, or does it include a case in which the bride was not a virgin, or even when a marriage had been made between relatives who were too close? Christian mission did not cancel Gentile marriages but allowed and even required that marriages between relatives that were too close be ended, as they were banned in the Torah (cf. 1 Corinthians 5:1). This is probably the sense of the ruling in Acts 15:29. At any rate, the Gospel of Luke formulates the words very clearly:

> Everyone who divorces his wife and marries another commits adultery, and he who marries a woman divorced from her husband commits adultery. (Luke 16:18)

According to this verse, a man commits adultery if he divorces his wife and marries again, but also if he marries a woman abandoned by her husband. Jesus' words radically deviated from the Torah ruling that she was free and had a document for it.

The Apostles' Teachings on Remarriage

Paul bans divorce by referring to Jesus' words:

> To the married I give this charge (not I, but the Lord): the wife should not separate from her husband (but if she does, she should remain unmarried or else be reconciled to her husband), and the husband should not divorce his wife. (1 Corinthians 7:10–11)

A Christian wife or husband must not leave her or his non-Christian spouse if the faith divides the family. Paul goes on to allow them to part ways, but neither of them is to marry another. According to Romans 7:1–3, death ends marriage. Then the widow is free for a new marriage. It is true that Paul himself prefers single life for widows, but here he openly says that this is his own opinion. He goes on enigmatically:

> But if the unbelieving partner separates, let it be so. In such cases the brother or sister is not enslaved. God has called you to peace. (1 Corinthians 7:15)

First, it is not easy to apply this passage to modern, Western Christian life. Who is meant by "unbelieving partner" if the majority of the nation is at least nominally Christian? Paul did not write to a church in which some were "born-again Christians" and the rest were not. The Corinthians knew very well who had converted to Christianity and who were Gentiles. But above all, it is not obvious what Paul meant by saying that "the brother or sister is not enslaved." Was he saying that a Christian wife is not bound to walk back to the house from which she has been thrown out and that the husband is not obliged to endlessly ask his wife to return if she has decided to leave him because of his new religion? Or is Paul saying that she or he is free to enter into a new marriage? We see how easily we unintentionally fill the gap left by Paul with our own ideas.

Remarriage and Early Christianity

Most early Christian texts strictly banned a new marriage if the former spouse was alive. Some writers also banned a second marriage for a widow. According to Athenagoras (AD 177), a remarried widow overlooks that not only the flesh but also the spirit connects the couple (*Plea for Christians*, 33:6). Tertullian claims that the Christian widow after her remarriage has two spouses—one in spirit and another in flesh (*De monogamia*, 10). Nevertheless, a second marriage was mostly allowed to widows, probably because it was allowed in the New Testament (Romans 7:1–3; 1 Timothy 5:14).

But what was allowed for widows was rarely, if ever, allowed if a person's spouse was still living. The *Shepherd of Hermas* requires the husband to divorce his adulterous wife but simultaneously considers it a severe sin if he remarries and makes repentance impossible for the first wife. Athenagoras says (177) that a second marriage is just a specious adultery (*Plea for Christians*, 33:3–4). The Council of Elvira (Canon 9) excommunicated a woman who left her husband and entered into marriage with another. Origen, however, said that some church leaders had allowed some women to remarry, and he did not completely reject it (*Commentary on Matthew*, 1:14–23). But the main line was crystal clear.

Reformation and Remarriage

Christian ideas slowly started to influence Western laws, and in many cases, over the centuries, they grew together. Marriage had always been a very important institution, and governments had also addressed how marriage was to be terminated. The medieval Roman Church did not principally allow divorce and remarriage, but it easily annulled marriages of noblemen and rich men and made them free for new love. The reformers clearly understood that this practice was defective. They did not have the same authority within their churches as the pope and bishops had in Rome to forbid divorce and remarriage but allow annulment, and this made divorce a problem, which they tried to solve by biblical interpretation. In his writing *Babylonian Captivity* (1520), Martin Luther admitted he was clueless and in deep trouble because of the conflict between papal law and the biblical material. People left their spouses, which left the pastor to wrestle with the problem. This led Luther to a little-known and still-less-accepted solution. He allowed Philip of Hesse, who had been led to marriage by his parents, to secretly take another wife, trying so to follow Old Testament models (1539). This step was simply wrong, but it shows how Luther tried to find a solution that would not offend the Word of God. The words of Jesus prevented Luther, unlike the Catholic authorities, from allowing divorce for the prince, as it was not allowed to ordinary Christians, especially because the wife had not committed adultery and it was not possible to throw her out. But the secret contract became public, and the scandal taught Luther biblical interpretation.

The unhappy odyssey was buried in the mud of history, but the problem was not. *Concordia: The Lutheran Confessions* only have one sentence about remarriage: Philip Melanchthon says in his Treatise on the Power and Primacy of the Pope,

> Also unjust is the tradition forbidding an innocent person to marry after divorce. (Treatise, paragraph 78)

This sentence was part of a vivid debate in the sixteenth century that cannot be opened here. As it stands, here it is far from clear. Of course, the one who has an extramarital affair is "guilty." But every married Christian knows how difficult it is to find a person "innocent" in the family. Nevertheless, Lutheran churches have sought "guilty" and "innocent" parties in marriages for centuries. This belongs to the past in most Western churches, and they rather allow anyone to marry anyone, and the pastors bless it as many times as they are asked. This looks similar to Roman Imperial times, when marriage simply secured the juridic side of the current sexual relationship. It requires some elasticity to combine this with Jesus' words. The current practice is not based on the Bible but on the fact that an originally radical movement has been amalgamated with middle-class society. This has not helped people in their tears of sorrow after they have left and been left.

It might be allowed for us to distinguish between two cases, although this distinction is admittedly nonbiblical. In the first case, a person reflects on a possible new marriage. In the second, she or he has already entered into it years or even decades ago and might even have children from this marriage. Jesus' words are very problematic in the former case. In the latter case, the first Christians in Corinth and elsewhere might help us with their experience. A Gentile entering the church may have entered and ended several marriages, but they were welcomed to the kingdom of mercy just as they were. Every divorce is a loss, and Jesus' own words make every new marriage after it very problematic, but a Christian is not obliged to look back and carry the loads Christ has carried to make her or him free.

Reflection Questions

- How similar is the current Western lifestyle to that of ancient Greece and Rome?

- Modern Christians face a conflict between the need to remarry and Jesus' prohibition. What are your thoughts?

- How does your church meet people who have gotten divorced and remarried?

11

We and the World: Sexual Morality in Our Context

These chapters have led us to walk with Paul to Corinth and ask what kind of family and sexual morals he encountered in the city inhabited by Greeks, Romans, and a Jewish minority. Paul's teaching in Corinth came to define the Christian creed when it comes to sexual ethics. But as we continue to grapple with these questions, we should also pay attention to Paul's profane contemporaries. Since the Christian religion has lost much of its traditional role in the Western world, the Corinth of Paul's time bears a striking resemblance to our world today.

Summary

The first converts in Corinth, like everywhere else, started to live by the new ethics. This relegated them to a small minority. They were, however, not alone: For centuries, Jewish sexual morals had been derived from the Holy Scriptures, now common to Christians. The Christians also adopted many

Jewish interpretations not explicitly written in the Scriptures. The path was beaten for the early church.

Classical antiquity knew effective means to reduce pregnancies with drugs affecting fertility and causing early abortion. If a baby was not welcome, she or he was possibly thrown out or killed for reasons that still resonate in the modern discourse on abortion. The child might have been disabled or born as a result of an extramarital relationship. She or he might have been of the wrong sex or simply not needed in a family that already had enough children. Authorities often worried about a low birth rate, and girls were abandoned so often that it made a bad situation worse. The governments of today know these problems all too well, and they are as clueless in dealing with them as their predecessors were two thousand years earlier. Low fertility decreases economic prospects in many countries, and hundreds of millions of girls have been aborted or exposed as infants in Asian countries.

Jewish religious authorities did not allow the exposure of children or abortion, and the Christians followed suit soon after the New Testament times. And while early Judaism did not completely ban contraception, the early church did so in the third century.

What might be most surprising to a modern reader is the liberties taken by Greek and Roman men before and during marriage. A free Roman man could have sex with his slave girls and boys; with his concubine; with women and men serving in banquets, baths, and brothels; and—as the cheapest and quickest option—with the poor living on the streets who were ready for paid sex in porticos. Such relations usually started as soon as a boy was physically able and went on during his marriage, although not necessarily under his wife's eyes. Some philosophers emphasized austerity, and it was not considered an honor to be led by pleasure. Nevertheless, repeated sexual intercourse did not tarnish a man's reputation in any way. But this did not apply to women.

The ancient world was often bisexual, but the Christian Church labeled homosexuality a sin. For two thousand years, it has quoted biblical texts from both the Old and New Testaments and thus followed the Jewish tradition.

Marriage was a very strong institution in the Greek and Roman worlds, and its goal was to produce lawful children and citizens. Practices to enter into marriage varied, but it was mostly considered a contract confirmed with a document. The contract could also be canceled, and divorce was possible, especially in Rome, for both men and women, as many times as they wanted. Divorce could happen for practically any reason, and it was rarely considered shameful. Christians, like their Jewish predecessors, valued marriage and banned sex before and outside of marriage. However, they deviated from their mother religion at two points because of Jesus' words. Whereas mainline Judaism considered marriage and procreation a duty, the early church also saw single life as a duty given by God and, after some centuries, even preferred it to marriage. Jewish religious authorities allowed men (and sometimes women) to divorce, and both partners could freely marry again, although not with their former spouses. Christians, due to Jesus' words, banned divorce and remarriage of both partners.

Greek and Roman sexual morals might shock a Christian reader. Nevertheless, we should not summarily label them "immoral." They had their moral codes, even though these codes differed from the Jewish or Christian ones. People had not turned into devils. There were rules and limits that were considered reasonable. Adultery, for example, was widely considered wrong and punishable. The postmodern Western societies are not so different in this regard. We also have moral codes. One thing is approved of, another is banned, and it would be important for a Christian who desires to understand his or her society to seek to understand these boundaries that are probably different among the young and the old. This is the only manner in which to engage people and not straw men.

Although many elements of Christian sexual ethics have faded in the modern world, some elements sit deeply in the Western mind. Pedophilia was not banned by laws, and female children were abandoned or killed much more often than boys in pre-Christian Europe. Today pedophiles are jailed, and, until now, Western thought has not allowed parents to abort or abandon children because of their gender, although it is common in many countries.

Some Reflections

The Christian Church is simultaneously living in the past, present, and future. We are not free to choose our way as we like. We also worship an awesome God, who draws us lines we should not cross. Of course, we need to study the Scripture and the Christian tradition. But we also need to grow ears to listen to not only people regularly coming to church but also those who have distanced themselves from our Christian values. This is the only manner in which we can honor the mission God has given us: to be a light in the world. We should be ready to discuss these topics with our fellow students, colleagues, and neighbors, but also with our family and friends. Common ethics are formed through listening, discussing, and supporting one another, not screaming on social media. It is time to display our treasures.

Western sexual ethics have been influenced by deep social evolutions. People used to live in the countryside on farms previously owned by their parents and grandparents. In such a community, a young man could not easily avoid his responsibility if a single girl became pregnant. It was easier in the cities, where industry needed a growing number of workers. But the decisive change came with the introduction of contraceptives that allowed women to live as men had always lived—to have premarital sex with numerous people without fear of pregnancy. As usual, it has taken decades for the new material innovations to change conventional behavior and ethics. In my home country, Finland, women still have fewer sexual partners than men, but that number has rapidly grown to be five times larger than it was only a few decades ago.

These sweeping changes tempt conservative Christians to pick and choose parts of Christian sexual ethics and to proclaim those sections with loud voices. A typical example has been homosexuality. But there is no lack of other issues common in modern society that contrast sharply with both the Old and New Testaments and Christian tradition. Christian sexual ethics should be considered in their entirety, not as a buffet where you can pick what you want. In Finland, abortion ends about 15 percent of pregnancies, premarital sex precedes most marriages, divorces are common, and devout Christians remarry despite Jesus' words. We are deeper in the mire than we understand. Is there still a family immune to such controversies?

Christians now live between the Bible and Hollywood. It is striking how ancient sexual ethics have retaken the territories they once lost. Attitudes that were considered reasonable before Christianity's rise are also in fashion after

Christianity's decline. The ubiquitousness of sex has seriously challenged the church.

The time has come to present the Christian counterchallenge and preach like the early church. Are people sure that moving from bed to bed makes a person happy? Then why are people having less sex now than they did a few decades ago? Why has the consumption of pornography exploded, distorting children's views on women and men? Why are divorces destroying families? And if sex is only physical fun, why does it still hurt to be betrayed or abandoned?

God's gifts can manifest in the form of a loving spouse who stays with you for decades, as the beautiful prayer of Tobias quoted above expresses. Or they can be children growing up in a safe environment. In the end, few things have changed in two thousand years. God has created us as men and women, put the need for love in our hearts, and established marriage for us. This is also what makes a mother or father embrace their baby, even if they have never heard our sermons. The path illuminated by the Scriptures used to call for people in Corinth, and it still calls for us, even though it was not an easy way to follow then, and it still is not today.

For generations, parents in Christian countries could count on schools and churches to teach traditional sexual ethics to their children. The secularization of societies has turned churches into battlefields between traditional and modern ways of life. The unitary Christian front collapsed rapidly, and the battle goes on only sporadically in some churches.

The battleground closest to each of us lies in our own hearts. The New Testament urges us to put off our "old self" and put on the new self God has given to us in Baptism (Romans 6; Ephesians 4). This battle has raged for centuries in every Christian heart, but today, it presents us with an extraordinary challenge. It is difficult to take a solitary stand against the enormous wave of unchristian ethics.

Ancient Jews had learned to live as a minority in the Mediterranean world. Even then, Gentile practices continued to lure children and youth. The Jewish solution was based on their own community, the synagogue, and teaching that was easily understandable. This model was adopted by the early Christian Church. Christians did not accept the Gentile ways of Corinth.

A convert to the new path was supported by his or her community. Indeed, for a single Christian, or a single family, the outside pressure has always been overwhelming. We need contacts with other Christians, families, and friends. We also need to be instructed, but more effective than listening to teachers and priests is the power of example. Every big sister and brother, every young couple, and every single person is a living witness of Christian ethics, just as every elderly couple staying together and working for their marriage is. We must again learn to live as a minority and seek trustworthy communities wherever we can find them.

No wonder especially that young Christians are perplexed about sexual identity—not only their own but also that of their friends. How are we to get along with people with a completely different code of ethics, which they consider an integral part of their identity? I would recommend caution. As a Christian, I am bound by what the Scripture says about love, sex, and marriage. But I also consider every human being as created and loved by God, regardless of his or her religion, ethics, or sexual identity. God loves everyone I meet, but He has also presented His treasures to me in the Bible, and I am ready to share them with everyone.

When Paul wrote the letter we know as 1 Corinthians, no one who had grown up in Corinth had been a Christian for more than five years. Every Gentile not taught in the synagogue had learned to live by the social morals presented in the previous chapters, and it is safe to assume that especially the men had had an adventurous past even by modern standards. Nevertheless, they were welcome to join the church and had to learn new habits. Paul's letters show the sparks flying. People made mistakes but started over again. How can we do our best to welcome the wounded who need a merciful Savior and a safe home?

Christian sexual ethics still means light in the darkness. Now we need to bring this light to people so it can lighten their own hearts and environments.

Reflection Questions

- What have you learned from reading this book?

- Christians are badly pulled between the morality of the Bible and the morality represented by Hollywood. What can we do to help our children and young people?

- Christians are often keen to address one part of Christian sexual morals, emphasize it, and stay silent on the most difficult problems. What are some examples of this? Why do you think this is the case?

- Do you still believe that traditional Christian sexual morals are competitive with social morals today? In other words, do they lead us in the right way?

TRANSLATIONS USED

Barclay, John M. G., trans. *Flavius Josephus: Translation and Commentary*. Vol. 10: *Against Apion*. Brill, 2007.

Charlesworth, James H., ed. *The Old Testament Pseudepigrapha*. 2 vols. Doubleday, 1983.

Demosthenes. "Against Neaera, 122." In *Demosthenes, with an English translation*. Translated by Norman W. DeWitt and Norman J. DeWitt. Harvard University Press, 1949.

Gellius, Aulus. *Attic Nights*. Books 1–5. Translated by J. C. Rolfe. Loeb Classical Library. Harvard University Press, 1927.

Holmes, Michael W., ed. and trans. *The Apostolic Fathers: Greek Texts and English Translations*. 3rd ed. Baker Academic, 2007.

Hunt, A. S. and C. C. Edgar, and D. L. Page, ed. and trans. *Select Papyri: Private Documents*. Volume 1. Loeb Classical Library. Harvard University Press, 1932.

Lieberman, Saul, ed. *Tosefta Ki-Feshutah: A Comprehensive Commentary on the Tosefta*. 8 vols. Jewish Theological Seminary of America, 1955.

Neusner, Jacob. *The Mishnah: A New Translation*. Yale University Press, 1991.

Percival, Henry R., ed. and trans. "The Synod of Gangra." In *The Nicene and Post Nicene Fathers*. Series 2. Volume 14. Wm. B. Eerdmans Publishing Company, 1983.

Philo. *Philo*. Translated by F. H. Colson and George Herbert Whitaker. Loeb Classical Library. Harvard University Press, 1966.

Pliny the Elder. *Natural History*. Vol. 8. Books 28–32. Translated by W. H. S. Jones. Loeb Classical Library. Harvard University Press, 1963.

Riley, Henry Thomas, trans. *The Comedies of Plautus*. G. Bell & Sons, 1913.

Roberts, Alexander, James Donaldson, and A. Cleveland Coxe, ed. and trans. *The Ante-Nicene Fathers*. Vol. 4. Wipf and Stock, 2022.

Suetonius. *Lives of the Caesars, Volume I: The Deified Julius. The Deified Augustus. Tiberius. Gaius Caligula*. Translated by J. C. Rolfe. Loeb Classical Library. Harvard University Press, 1914.